TOERIST MODERNIST

Gerlin Heestermans

Walking along modernist architecture in Belgium

LUSTER

This collection of modernist architecture walking tours has been many years in the making, long before I actually even planned to write this book. All that time I was always on the look-out for forgotten or little-known modernist buildings in Belgium, spending every free moment of my time on research and documentation. The result? A folder full of Excel files and a Google Map featuring thousands of saved locations. I call it my passion, some would say that it borders on the obsessive.

After I started to share my finds on Instagram, people often asked me where they could find that specific building. That is how the idea of creating my first walking guide was born, during the first lockdown in 2020. Soon after, in early 2021, Luster asked me if I'd be interested in creating several of these guides, to be combined into a book. At first I was hesitant, because I felt like I didn't have the knowledge required to take on a project of this size. At the same time, though, I started to realise that it was necessary as some of the places that I had documented disappeared not much later. Nothing lasts forever, so better to do something about it as soon as possible! This forced me to conclude that there is no time like the present and that irons are best struck when they're hot. Off I went, and the rest, as they say, is history!

I have no regrets as my decision paved the way for many experiences and encounters that I would've otherwise missed out on. Staying in a modernist icon for a week? Check. Being invited to lunch? Check. Getting to take a look behind every single door? Check. Hearing compelling, personal stories from both owners and architects or family members of those architects? Check. Discovering dreamy interiors, maintained by passionate and patient owners? Check!

Telling people you're writing a book literally and figuratively opens doors. That does not mean, however, that the owners of the houses that are featured in this book will open their doors to everyone (and that includes me). So, please be mindful of people's privacy when walking past their homes and don't trespass!

My goal with this book was to show you just how rich and diverse the architectural landscape of a tiny country like Belgium is, by focussing specifically on that radical, modernist era that lies so close to my heart. It's also worth noting that most of these buildings are not listed, meaning they can be demolished or renovated beyond recognition whenever an owner sees fit. As this happens quite often, I cannot promise that every building will still be as described.

At the time of writing, I didn't have my driving licence yet. I am a firm believer in using public transport as much as possible anyway, so the starting points are always close to a train, tram or bus stop.

Here's hoping that this book will contribute to increasing appreciation for this beautiful and valuable heritage, and that you will be just as amazed and surprised to discover it as I was.

How to use this book

Each chapter consists of:

- words telling you where to go and what you're looking at;
- photos showing you what to look for;
- a map to help you navigate;
- a list of addresses (strictly in case of emergency – figuring it out for yourself is much more fun!);
- the length of the route in kilometres.

The length of the route is the walking distance between the starting point (usually a train station or a bus or tram stop) and the last stop.

Mariakerke (Ghent)

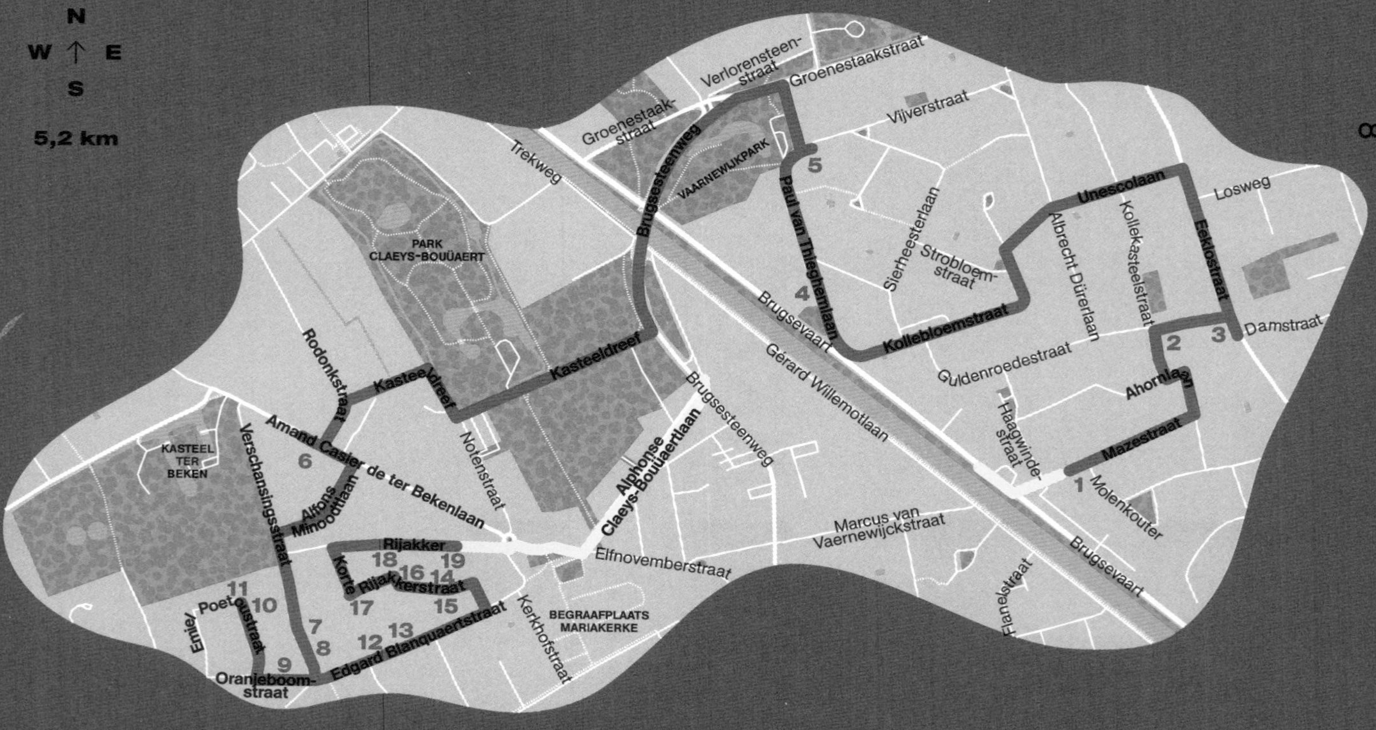
N
W E
S
5,2 km
Verlorensteen-
straat
Groenestaakstraat
Groenestaak-
straat
Vijverstraat
Trekweg
VAARNEWIJKPARK
Brugsesteenweg
Paul van Thieghemlaan
Sierheesterlaan
Strobloem-
straat
Unescolaan
Albrecht Dürerlaan
Kollekasteelstraat
Eeklostraat
Losweg
Damstraat
Guldenroedestraat
Ahornlaan
Mazestraat
Molenkouter
Haagwinde-
straat
Kollebloemstraat
Brugsevaart
Gérard Willemotlaan
PARK
CLAEYS-BOUÜAERT
Kasteeldreef
Rodonkstraat
Brugsesteenweg
Alphonse
Claeys-Bouüaertlaan
Amand Casier de ter Bekenlaan
Notenstraat
KASTEEL
TER
BEKEN
Verschansingsstraat
Alfons
Minoodtlaan
Rijakker
Korte Rijakkerstraat
Elfnovemberstraat
Marcus van
Vaernewijckstraat
Flanelstraat
Kerkhofstraat
BEGRAAFPLAATS
MARIAKERKE
Emiel
Poetoustraat
Oranjeboom-
straat
Edgard Blanquaertstraat
1
2
3
4
5
6
7
8
9
10
11
12
13
14
15
16
17
18
19

1 Mazestraat 46
Dan Grootaert
1959

2 Guldenroedestraat 40-42
Luk Van den Broeck
1969

3 Eeklostraat 53
Joannes Cloostermans
1932

4 Paul van Tieghemlaan 24
Emil Buyse
1963

5 Vijverstraat 2
Louis Geirnaert
1966

6 Amand Casier de ter Bekenlaan 35
Marcel Dietens
1956

7 Verschansingsstraat 6
Dan Craet
1955

8 Verschansingsstraat 4
Dan Craet
1955

9 Verschansingsstraat 1
Dan Craet
1958

10 Emiel Poetoustraat 23
Dan Craet
1960

11 Emiel Poetoustraat 21
Dan Craet
1961

12 Edgard Blancquaertstraat 28
Georges Cosyns
1938

13 Edgard Blancquaertstraat 18
Dan Craet
1955

14 Korte Rijakkerstraat 9
Olivier Nowé & René Heyvaert
1958

15 Korte Rijakkerstraat 19
Olivier Nowé & René Heyvaert
1959

16 Korte Rijakkerstraat 34
Dan Craet
1958

17 Korte Rijakkerstraat 16
Dan Craet
1955

18 Rijakker 19
Victor Laureys
1959

19 Rijakker 11
Olivier Nowé & René Heyvaert
1957

Originally, Mariakerke was a rural area, split in two by the Ghent-Bruges Canal. From the early 1800s, labourers and middle-class people moved to this suburb, which is located to the west of Ghent. Later, rich townspeople also discovered the area, building their country homes there. The many castles around Mariakerke are a reminder of this trend. After the Second World War, Ghent's population grew faster than ever, meaning housing – and thus many modernist dwellings – had to be built to accommodate them.

On this route you'll explore both banks of the canal, focusing mainly on the post-war period, with only two interbellum buildings thrown in the mix.

You start off on the eastern side of the canal. Get off the bus at Mariakerke Mazestraat and walk down Mazestraat, where the former home and studio of glass artist Armand Blondeel awaits at number 46, concealed behind lush greenery (**1**). Blondeel specialised in the design of stained-glass windows for architectural projects, among others, creating several for his own home too. He chose to work with his good friend, the architect Dan Grootaert, for the design of this house, giving him carte blanche. Grootaert went all out, combining volumes with different materials, resulting in this playful design.

1. Mazestraat 46, Dan Grootaert (1959)

Continue to walk down Mazestraat to Ahornlaan, where you turn left. After the bend, turn right on Kollekasteelstraat, then right again on Guldenroedestraat. Immediately on your right, at number 40, you will find a double home, designed by Luc Van den Broeck (**2**). Compared to the Grootaert house you just saw, this design is much simpler, minimalistic and even more private, with almost no openings or windows facing the street.

2. Guldenroedestraat 40-42, Luk Van den Broeck (1969)

Walk on until you reach Eeklostraat and spot number 53, by Joannes Cloostermans, on the corner (**3**) – this is the first interbellum building on this route. As it's so well kept and several other houses from that era have been preserved intact on this street, looking at this villa is a bit like being transported back in time. As you walked towards the house, you may have also noticed the stairwell at the rear, which is completely encased in glass (although it looks a bit heavier now, because of the renovated frames, which are darker in colour and thicker). Imagine being able to walk up those stairs to the roof that served as a sun terrace – it doesn't get much dreamier than that!

Go left onto Eeklostraat, then left again on Unescolaan, which turns into Kollebloemstraat. To stay on Kollebloemstraat, turn left at the end of the street, then continue walking until this street turns into Paul van Tieghemlaan. Number 24 (**4**), by Emil Buyse, has been renovated, but the original features of the façade have been preserved. A more toned-down version of the Expo 58 style, this house is still spectacular because of the combination of different volumes.

4. Paul van Tieghemlaan 24, Emil Buyse (1963)

Keep walking until Paul van Tieghemlaan turns into Vijverstraat and stop at number 2, a design by Louis Geirnaert from 1966 (**5**). Geirnaert was from Eeklo and his oeuvre is extensively covered in the chapter on this city. His take on modernism was exuberant, combining materials, colours, and a certain graphic affinity that was very much his own. This example may seem minimalist by comparison, but the devil's in the detail: notice the use of different levels, and alternating materials such as Glasal and wood.

5. Vijverstraat 2, Louis Geirnaert (1966)

Now it's time to cross the canal. Turn around and go right on Paul van Tieghemlaan, then left on Groenestaakstraat until it turns into Brugsesteenweg. Cross the bridge, then take the first on your right, Kasteeldreef, and keep walking until you hit a fork in the road, where you turn right. After the next bend, turn left onto Rodonkstraat, which intersects with Amand Casier de ter Bekenlaan, where you turn right and walk to number 35 (**6**). While Marcel Dietens may not be quite as well known as his peers, he succeeds in ticking all the boxes here with this colourful interpretation of the Expo 58 style.

6. Amand Casier de ter Bekenlaan 35, Marcel Dietens (1956)

Turn back and walk down Amand Casier de ter Bekenlaan, taking the first on your right, Alfons Minoodtlaan. At the top of the street, turn left onto Verschansingsstraat. You are now entering Dan(iël) Craet territory. Dan Craet is perhaps the most important name in post-war modernism in

Ghent, and this was his playground. Back in the 1950s, this area was owned by the Nowé family, whose son Olivier happened to be an architect. Over time, it got subdivided into separate parcels that were sold to private clients. Under the sales contract, they were obliged to work with Nowé for the construction of their homes. This allowed Nowé and his team to build an entire district in their own style, inspired by the Californian Case Study Houses. Nowé collaborated with René Heyvaert, whose ideas on cheap, modular construction he shared and which they wanted to realise here. However, the municipal department and some of their clients found their ideas far too radical, which explains why they had to slightly adapt their plans.

Craet came on board because his wife knew the Nowés. As such, he designed most of the houses in this neighbourhood. He worked with Frida Burssens, his wife, who was also a designer and decorator. She is responsible for the bold colour combinations in the interiors and exteriors of her husband's designs.

The collaboration between Burssens and Craet is especially apparent in the house built for Frida's father, Amaat Burssens, at Verschansingsstraat 6 (**7**). This light, open bungalow, which is tucked away behind lush green plantings, obviously takes a page from Scandinavian modernism. Amaat (who was a linguist specialising in African languages) had a small museum for his private collection in the building in the garden. When Amaat decided to move out, the couple moved into this house. After Frida's death, the house stayed in the family and was beautifully preserved. The typical kitchen with two-way cupboards (manufactured by another Ghent icon, Van Den Berghe-Pauvers) has been preserved as is, among other things.

7. Verschansingsstraat 6, Dan Craet (1955)

Earlier, Burssens and Craet lived next door at number 4 (**8**), which has since undergone extensive changes. 8. Verschansingsstraat 4, Dan Craet (1955)

Now cross the street to number 1 (**9**) for another gem by Dan Craet. As you continue your tour, you'll be seeing many more designs by Craet, so it's interesting to pay attention to the details, as they are what sets the different houses apart and makes them unique. The house at number 1 is especially remarkable because of the grand entrance with a visible staircase behind tall windows that span the entire height of the façade.

9. Verschansingsstraat 1, Dan Craet (1958)

Turn right onto Oranjeboomstraat, then immediately right again onto Emiel Poetoustraat. Many of the people that acquired a parcel in this neighbourhood were quite progressive. They liked the modern, innovative designs of the houses that they were building. One such proprietor was sculptor Emiel Poetou – the street has been named after him – who lived at number 23 (**10**). The façade is adorned with a sculpture by Poetou (although the current owners changed the colour scheme). You can find more of his sculptures in the nearby Westerbegraafplaats cemetery. Right next door, at number 21 (**11**), is another expressive Craet design.

10. Emiel Poetoustraat 23, Dan Craet (1960)

11. Emiel Poetoustraat 21, Dan Craet (1961)

Turn back and go left, returning to Oranjeboomstraat, which turns into Edgard Blancquaertstraat further on. At number 28 you can find the second and last interbellum building on this route (**12**), from 1936. The architect Georges Cosyns clearly had a soft spot for the Amsterdam School style. This is apparent in the shape of the house, among other things, which is very different from other houses in this neighbourhood.

At number 18, we have another Craet house (**13**). This one is part of the ensemble of buildings, that he designed in 1955 for the plot owned by the Nowé family. Here, his juxtaposition of different materials is especially noteworthy, in the combination of exposed and painted brick and wood. Unfortunately, the façade has been stripped of many of its original elements (such as the trademark Craet garage door handle you'll come across later), but it is still a great testament to Craet's earlier work.

13. Edgard Blancquaertstraat 18, Dan Craet (1955)

Take the next street on your left, Korte Rijakkerstraat. As Nowé-Heyvaert and/or Craet designed the entire street, you should feel as if you're on familiar terrain by now. Most of the façades have been modernised and lack that original spirit, but fortunately some have been preserved. Number 9 (**14**) still belongs to members of the Nowé family and is partly intact. Fun fact: the house was actually built (as in: with bare hands, not designed) by Nowé's students at the time. This would not have been such a slog, given that he worked with ready-made materials for the most part.

Here the difference between the Nowé-Heyvaert designs and Craet's designs is very distinct. Whereas Craet tended towards ornamentation, Nowé and Heyvaert constructed basic, cheap, modular buildings of a temporary nature, that were adapted to their surroundings and occupants. They sought to create a model for modern living, a near-utopia. As you may have guessed, the materials they used were not the most sustainable and many of them did not withstand the test of time.

Number 19 (**15**) is an especially interesting example. In view of the wear and tear, the owners carried out a thoughtful renovation, retaining the original structure, but making the building future-proof with some practical adjustments (such as insulation). At the same time, they restored the house with references to Nowé & Heyvaert's designs, using vertical slats for the eaves and corrugated iron for the roof. Their restoration efforts are a beautiful tribute to Nowé-Heyvaert.

Across the street, at number 34, you'll find another Craet design (**16**). Compared with the other Craets you've seen so far, this house is different in that it has a bare façade. The plans indicate that it was supposed to be painted white, just like the other houses you've seen. For some reason, this never happened, and the result is striking. The yellow door features a recognisable handle, a typical 1950s design feature. The colour scheme was used both outside and inside the house and is most visible in the kitchen.

16. Korte Rijakkerstraat 34, Dan Craet (1958)

Continue walking to number 16 (**17**), another beautiful example of Craet's characteristic style. Apart from the studio that was added later (behind the house, not visible from the street), everything has been preserved as it was in 1955. Notice the wonderful combination of materials, the white painted brick, the colourful doors (thanks to Frida Burssens) and, as previously mentioned, Craet's trademark garage door handle.

17. Korte Rijakkerstraat 16, Dan Craet (1955)

Keep walking down Korte Rijakkerstraat, then turn right onto Rijakker, until you reach number 19 (**18**). Besides Nowé, Heyvaert, and Craet, there were several other modern architects who built houses in this area, such as Victor Laureys. Although he was originally from Lokeren and most of his oeuvre can be found in that town, Laureys really found his style with this dwelling from 1959. In this family home, which was clearly influenced by the Expo 58 aesthetic, he has combined a playful bas-relief, with a colourful façade and different volumes. A wonderful sight.

18. Rijakker 19, Victor Laureys (1959)

Your last stop is at number 11 (**19**): a cosy home by Nowé-Heyvaert, of which the layout and some of the original features have been preserved.

19. Rijakker 11, Olivier Nowé & René Heyvaert (1957)

To get to the bus stop, continue walking down Rijakker until you reach the roundabout and take the second street on your right, Mariakerkeplein. Next, turn left onto Alphonse Claeys-Bouüaertlaan. At the end of the street, take a left on Brugsesteenweg. The Mariakerke Post bus stop is immediately on your left.

Rijakker 11, Olivier Nowé & René Heyvaert (1957)

Rijakker 11, Olivier Nowé & René Heyvaert (1957)

Charleroi

Petite Ceinture de Charleroi
Rue de la Broucheterre
Bd Jacques Bertrand
Rue Isaac
13
Bd Frans Dewandre
Bd Zoé Drion
Rue Huart Chapel
Chau. de Bruxelles
Petite Ceinture de Charleroi
PALAIS DES BEAUX ARTS
Bd Solvay
Rue Chavannes
PALAIS DES EXPOSITIONS DE CHARLEROI
14
Rue Neuve
Bd Paul Janson
Bd Joseph II
Av. de L'Europe
Bd Jacques Bertrand
Rue de la Science
Bd Alfred de Fontaine
Rue Turenne
Place Charles II
10
12
Bd Pierre Mayence
Petite Ceinture de Charleroi
Av. Des Alliés
Rue de la Digue
Rue de France
Rue d'Orléans
11
Av. du Général Michel
15
Bd de l'Yser
16
Rue du Grand Central
9
Bd Audent
PARC REINE ASTRID
8
Bd Audent
7
Rue Willy Ernst
Bd Pierre Mayence
Bd Joseph Tirou
Rue de Montigny
Quai Paul Verlaine
6
Bd Joseph Tirou
Rue Jean Monnet
5
Rue du Pont Neuf
Rue Olof Palme
Rue Arthur Regniers
Petite Ceinture de Charleroi
Av Gillieaux
Quai Paul Verlaine
3
Rue de l'Ecluse
4
LA SAMBRE
1
Quai Arthur Rimbaud
Quai de la Gare du S
Quai Arthur Rimbaud
Petite Ceinture de Charleroi
2
CHARLEROI-CENTRAL
Av. Marius Meurée
Rue de la Villette
Rue De La Villette

N

W ↑ **E**

S

5 km

1 Quai Arthur Rimbaud 5
Marcel Leborgne
1933

2 Quai de la Gare du Sud 1
Paul Nouille & Henry van de Velde
1933

3 Boulevard Joseph Tirou 221
Paul Hayot
1960

4 Boulevard Joseph Tirou 227
Paul Hayot
1960

5 Boulevard Joseph Tirou 167
Simon Brigode & Jules Laurent
1950

6 Boulevard Joseph Tirou 139
Pol Ongenae & Henri Leborgne
1956

7 Rue Adolphe Biarent 1
Joseph André
1954

8 Boulevard Audent 26
Jacques Depelsenaire
1964

9 Boulevard Audent 45
Joseph André
1929

10 Rue de la Science 12
unknown

11 Avenue du Général Michel 2
Simon Brigode & Jacques Depelsenaire
1963

12 Avenue du Général Michel 13
Marcel Depelsenaire
1936

13 Boulevard Frans Dewandre

14 Place du Manège 1
Joseph André
1957

15 Boulevard de l'Yser 7
unknown
1960s
(open Tuesday to Saturday)

16 Rue du Grand Central 29
unknown
1950s
(open Tuesday to Saturday)

Charleroi boasts a vast array of impressive architecture because of its industrial past (coal mining and steel industry). In terms of population, it is the third-largest city in Belgium, and the largest one in Wallonia. Despite this, Charleroi feels more like a large village, rather than a bustling city. Perhaps this has got something to do with the fact that the city lacks a university.

The many artificial hills that surround Charleroi (called “terrils” in French) lend the city its unique character. After the closing of the mines, Charleroi fell into a state of disrepair, which is apparent when looking at the architecture, which is often run-down. But don’t worry, there’s still more than enough left that is worth seeing. On this route you’ll be exploring a sort of best-of, starring buildings by the architects who shaped Charleroi as we know it today.

Exit through the main entrance of Charleroi-Central railway station and walk towards the Sambre river. Stay on this bank and take a right, following Quai de la Gare du Sud along the water. Beyond the Roi Baudouin bridge you should have a perfect view of a Charleroi icon: the old De Heug (**1**) piano store, that was designed by Marcel Leborgne in 1933. Following a recent restoration, the façade and lettering are gleaming like never before, offering a warm welcome to the city. 1. Quai Arthur Rimbaud 5, Marcel Leborgne (1933)

Continue your walk along the water until you reach 1, Quai de la Gare du Sud (**2**), just before the roundabout. Given its proximity to the railway station, it will come as no surprise that it was built to house offices of the SNCB, Belgium's national railway company. In those days, the SNCB employed its own in-house architect, Paul Nouille. For this project he chose to collaborate with none other than Henry van de Velde, the pioneer of the modern movement in Belgium, whose style is all over this building.

At the roundabout, take the first street on your left and cross the bridge, then immediately take a right onto Quai Arthur Rimbaud, which curves to the left and changes into Boulevard Joseph Tirou. Keep going, then cross the busy street to number 221 (**3**), on the corner of Rue Fernande Volral. At the opposite end, right across Rue Fernande Volral, you'll find number 227 (**4**). Both buildings were designed by Paul Hayot, who graduated just five years prior to building these beauties. With these two buildings, you're squarely in the playful, colourful Expo 58 era. Number 221 features red Glasal and concrete panels, combining to create a rhythmic façade that's reminiscent of an abstract painting. It's worth elaborating on Glasal here, as this material is often used in post-war modernist architecture, and you'll spot it often during these walks. A Belgian invention, Glasal panels are made from asbestos cement, and are coated with a top layer of colourfast enamel, giving them their bright hue. The colourful panels can be frequently found on buildings from the 1950s and 1960s, and are a big part of the Expo 58 aesthetic.

3. Boulevard Joseph Tirou 221, Paul Hayot (1960)

Number 227, on the other hand, features blue panels and is remarkable for its shape, with a characteristic butterfly roof and pilotis (freestanding columns that raise the structure off the ground).

From number 221's main entrance, turn right and walk to the roundabout. Cross the roundabout and stay on Boulevard Joseph Tirou. You'll soon see number 167 (**5**) loom up ahead, with, on the corner of the main façade, its vibrant bas-relief depicting workers at the feet of the Virgin Mary and the words "Notre Maison" ("Our House") spelled out above her head. Predating the playful 1950s buildings of your previous stop by just 10 years, these former offices of the Christian workers movement are completely different in spirit. This imposing building exudes a certain grandeur. Simon Brigode and Jules Laurent, the building's architects, managed to incorporate multiple works of art into their design. In addition to the bas-relief, there are also frescoes of workmen in the cafe on the ground floor by Zéphir Busine and Georges Boulmant. So do pop in if the cafe's open and have a look around! 5. Boulevard Joseph Tirou 167, Simon Brigode & Jules Laurent (1950)

On to the last stop on this boulevard: Galerie Bernard at number 139 (**6**). Once a lively covered passage full of shops, this arcade is now mostly deserted. Luckily most of the period details have been preserved, with the glass ceiling being the most striking feature.

Boulevard Joseph Tirou 167, frescoes by Zéphir Busine and Georges Boulmant (1950)

Walk through the gallery and turn left on Rue de Montigny, which turns into Rue de la Montagne almost immediately. Climb up the hill and take the first street on your right. Follow Rue du Palais until the end, where it turns into Rue Adolphe Biarent at the bend. Your next stop is here, at number 1: the Conservatoire Arthur Grumiaux (**7**). Joseph André already had quite the resume when he designed this building in 1954, given that he started working as an architect in the early 1900s. André embraced the coming and going of styles and made eclecticism his thing, drawing eagerly on both the modern and the classical, as you can see in this music academy. Another characteristic of his work is the frequent collaboration with local artists, and the building is a fine example of this. In the lobby you can spot a monumental sculpture by Charles De Rouck as well as marvellous stained-glass windows by an unknown designer in the corridor behind it.

7. Conservatoire Arthur Grumiaux, Rue Adolphe Biarent 1, sculpture: Charles De Rouck (1954)

Follow Rue Adolphe Biarent round the bend, then turn right onto Boulevard Audent. At number 26 (**8**) you will come across the first in a set of buildings by Charleroi-born Jacques Depelsenaire, whose work features heavily on the rest of this route. The son of the architect Marcel Depelsenaire, Jacques was inspired by the radically modern, post-war American architecture that prioritised functionalism above all else. In 1948, he won the prestigious Prix de Rome, going on to have a fruitful international career. Fortunately, he also completed several projects in his hometown. This block of flats is one of his later works and a good example of the functionalist style, although the use of different materials on the façade and the graphic steel grille also attest to the artistic quality of his work.

8. Boulevard Audent 26, Jacques Depelsenaire (1964)

Across the road, at number 45 (**9**), you can find another example of Joseph André's versatile style.

From number 45, turn left and then take the first street on your left, Rue d'Orléans, then turn right onto Rue de la Science. At number 12 (**10**), on the corner with Rue Emile Tumelaire, you'll see another example of this optimistic, playful 1950s architecture, once again featuring the colour blue.

10. Rue de la Science 12, unknown (1950s-1960s)

With your back to the building, turn left onto Rue Emile Tumelaire and walk to the corner of Boulevard Alfred de Fontaine. On this corner you can find what is perhaps Jacques Depelsenaire's masterpiece: the Charleroi Palais de Justice or Law Courts (**11**), which he designed in the late 1960s. The site is vast and it's worth wandering around if you have the time as there are many striking period details on which you can feast your eyes. Check out the sculpture next to the side entrance

(Boulevard Alfred de Fontaine), the canopy at the main entrance (Avenue du Général Michel), and the sculptures on the façade next to it. 11. Avenue du Général Michel 2, Simon Brigode & Jacques Depelsenaire (1963)

Continue walking down Rue Emile Tumelaire until you arrive at the corner of Avenue du Général Michel. Turn left and walk to number 13 (**12**). Depelsenaire's father Marcel designed this building, and it's obvious that you've travelled back in time, to a different era altogether: the interbellum. And what a well-preserved stunner this is. The glimmering tiles, the brickwork in different colours, the grille on the door, and the lettering: everything has been lovingly restored and it is a joy to behold. During the First World War, Depelsenaire was deported to the Netherlands. He returned to Charleroi, inspired by the architecture that he had seen there. The influence of the Amsterdam School is particularly apparent here. 12. Avenue du Général Michel 13, Marcel Depelsenaire (1936)

Cross the roundabout to Boulevard Zoé Drion and keep on walking until it turns into Boulevard Frans Dewandre (**13**), which basically doubles as an open-air museum. There's a lot to see here, so give yourself some time to take it all in. Several of these buildings (numbers 1, 3, and 14) were designed by one and the same architect: Marcel Leborgne. He and his brother Henri (one of the architects of the arcade that you just walked through) definitely took after their father Hector Leborgne, who was also an architect. Although the brothers developed opposing styles – Marcel was radically modern, while Henri was more conservative – they would go on to collaborate on several projects. Number 3 on this street originally was the house and practice of a doctor, which also featured Marcel Leborgne's renowned built-in furniture. Unfortunately, the façade has been altered quite a bit since, but you can imagine how striking it must've looked back in 1937 if you use your imagination. Leborgne's masterpiece, however, is Charleroi's Reine Astrid maternity hospital, which he designed around 1935. With its pink and black tiles, curved windows, and a colourful interior with stunning stained-glass art, this building was considered a true highlight of modernist architecture both in Belgium and beyond. In the 1980s, the hospital, which lacked modern equipment, lost a large part of its clientele, culminating in its demolition in 1987. Even though you can no longer see it, it would be wrong not to mention it here as it was such a groundbreaking, gorgeous design. In fact, while you're at it, google it now!

13. Boulevard Frans Dewandre 3, Marcel Leborgne (1937)

On to the rest of the route then. Turn around, cross over to the other side of the street, and take the first street on your right, Rue Léon Bernus. Turn right onto Rue Isaac, then take the second street on your left, Rue Zénobe Gramme. Continue walking until it turns into Rue Chavannes, and then turn right onto Place du Manège. You should now

Palais des Beaux Arts, Place du Manège 1, Joseph André (1957)

see the new wing of the Palais des Beaux Arts (**14**) in front of you. Walk to the older wing on the left and marvel at the building's absolute grandeur. You're not wrong in spotting similarities to the conservatory, because Joseph André designed both buildings. The seamless integration of art and architecture reaches new heights here. The building used to be home to a museum as well, which was closed several years ago. Nowadays, it is only open to the public for theatrical and other cultural productions, so you can't just walk in. It pays, though, to peek through the windows: you should be able to spot a sculpture by Marino Marini in the entrance hall. Hidden from view are a mural by René Magritte, sculptures by Alphonse Darville, a painting by Ossip Zadkine, gorgeous period furniture, etc.

14. Palais des Beaux Arts, Place du Manège 1, Joseph André (1957)

From buildings by some of the Carolo (as the people of Charleroi are called) greats, you now move into more uncharted territory. Walk down Boulevard Jacques Bertrand, then turn left onto Boulevard de l'Yser and stop at number 7 (**15**). The overall architecture of the building is a mix of different elements, but it's the interior on the right-hand side that deserves your attention. This optician's practice hasn't changed since it opened in the 1960s and the furniture and accessories are absolutely delightful. The current owner of this family business has vowed to maintain the interior exactly as is. You can visit it during opening hours, from Tuesday till Saturday.

15. Boulevard de l'Yser 7, unknown (1960s)

Turn around and walk back down Boulevard de l'Yser, which eventually turns into Avenue des Alliés. Turn left onto Rue de la Digue, then right onto Rue de Louvain, and left again onto Rue du Grand Central.

Boulevard de l'Yser 7, unknown (1960s)

Number 29 (**16**) is home to another well-preserved interior, this time from the 1950s. You can also visit it during opening hours, from Tuesday till Saturday. Even if you're a vegetarian, you can't help but notice how beautiful this butcher's store is with its original counter, door, tiles, and more. Absolutely delightful!

16. Rue du Grand Central 29, unknown (1950s)

Continue your walk until you reach a roundabout, then take the second street on your right, Rue Jean Monnet, which will lead you back to the river. The train station is on the opposite bank.

Rue du Grand Central 29, unknown (1950s)

Kortrijk

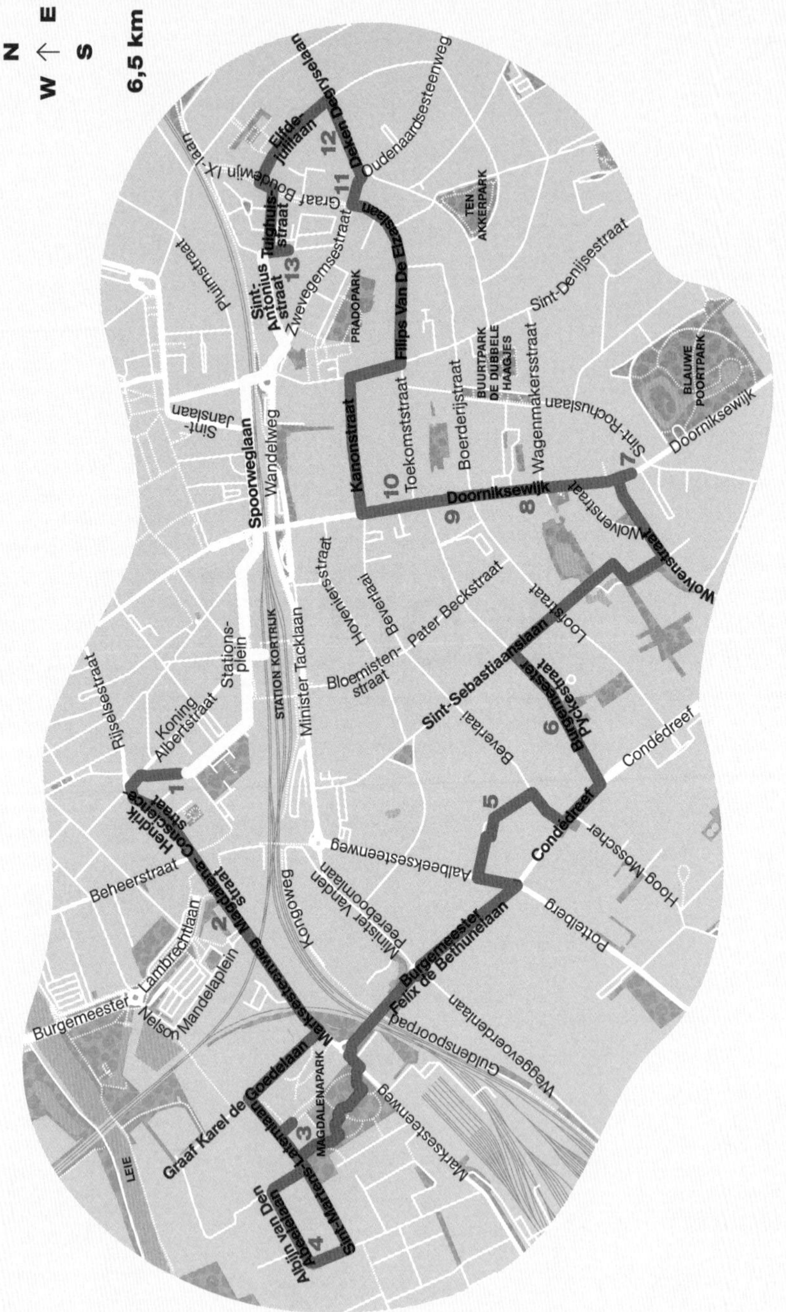

N
W
E
S
6,5 km
Deken Degryselaan
Elfde-Julilaan
Oudenaardsesteenweg
Graaf Boudewijn IX-laan
TEN AKKERPARK
Tulpinstraat
Sint-Antonius straat
Tulphuis-straat
Zwevegemsestraat
PRADOPARK
Filips Van De Elzelaan
Sint-Denijsestraat
BUURTPARK DE DUBBELE HAAGJES
Wagenmakersstraat
Boerderijstraat
Toekomststraat
Kanonstraat
BLAUWE POORTPARK
Sint-Rochuslaan
Doorniksewijk
Sint-Janslaan
Spoorweglaan
Wandelweg
Wolvenstraat
Loofstraat
Pater Beckstraat
Beverlaai
Hovenierstraat
Minister Tacklaan
STATION KORTRIJK
Stationsplein
Bloemistenstraat
Sint-Sebastiaanslaan
Burgemeester Nolfstraat
Burgemeester Pyckestraat
Condédreef
Rijselsestraat
Koning Albertstraat
Hendrik Conscience-straat
Magdalenastraat
Beheerstraat
Aalbeeksesteenweg
Hoog Mosscher
Kongoweg
Minister Vanden Peereboomlaan
Burgemeester Felix de Bethunelaan
Pottelberg
Lambrechtlaan
Nelson Mandelaplein
Burgemeester
Marksesteenweg
Guldensporenpad
Weggevoerdenlaan
Graaf Karel de Goedelaan
MAGDALENAPARK
Sint-Martens-Latemlaan
Albijn Van Den Abeelelaan
LEIE
1
2
3
4
5
6
7
8
9
10
11
12
13

1 Roeland Saverystraat 18
Jean Van Coppenolle
1958

2 Magdalenastraat 34
François Langeraert
1937

3 Sint-Martenslatemlaan 1
Paul Felix, Jan Tanghe, Jan De Jaegere, Christian Van der Plaetse
1960

4 Skatchkoffwijk (Konstant Permekelaan etc.)
Jan De Jaegere
1964

5 Beverlaaihof 5
Dan Craet
1961

6 Burgemeester Pyckestraat
André De Smedt
1963

7 Doorniksewijk 187
Poly Scherpereel
1930

8 Doorniksewijk 136A
Werner Van Spranghe
1930s

9 Doorniksewijk 84
Poly Scherpereel
1937

10 Doorniksewijk 31
Jan Robert Vanhoenacker
1931

11 Oudenaardsesteenweg 5
unknown
1930s

12 Deken Degryselaan 3, 13, 15, 16, 19, 25

13 Rijkswachtstraat 5
Willem Dutoit, Pierre A. Pauwels, Werner Van Spranghe
1940

Kortrijk has a rich (in every sense of the word) history that extends all the way back to the Roman Empire. The city flourished in the Middle Ages, with the production of flax and wool, connecting it to both England and France. Today, the textile industry still plays an important part in Kortrijk's economy.

During both World Wars, Kortrijk was partly destroyed. Qualifying this as "fortunate" would be silly, but as things stand, the space that was so brutally created did pave the way for the construction of more modern architecture on the city's ruins. Though the city is typically renowned for its medieval heritage, today's walking tour zooms in on a different era in architectural history.

Exit the Kortrijk train station and turn left onto Tolstraat, then right onto Conservatoriumplein (this is a street). Continue walking, leaving Casinoplein on your right, and at the top of the street, turn right onto Roeland Saverystraat. Have a look at numbers 16 and 18 (**1**), which are completely different in style, but are both great examples of post-war modernism. Number 18 is especially remarkable for its functionalism. Jean Van Coppenolle designed this house for a doctor, who had his consultation room on the ground floor, with the kitchen and living room being on the first floor, and the bedrooms on the second floor. He used very modern materials for that era (1958) and the façade still feels current. Van Coppenolle travelled extensively through the US and was inspired by architects such as Craig Ellwood and Pierre Koenig. Closer to home, he also took inspiration from the French architect Jean Prouvé, who often used "poor" or economic materials, like Van Coppenolle. Like his colleague Willy Van Der Meeren, Van Coppenolle was a socialist architect, designing affordable housing for the middle-class. For this house, however, he had a larger budget to work with, spending it on qualitative materials such as marble for the floors and using concrete and wood for the monumental staircase. On the first floor there's also a gorgeous, custom-built room divider.

Walk to the end of the street, turn left towards the roundabout and take the first street on your left, Hendrik Consciencestraat. Continue to walk down

Roeland Saverystraat 18, Jean Van Coppenolle (1958)

Roeland Saverystraat 18, Jean Van Coppenolle (1958)

this street until it becomes Magdalenastraat and you reach number 34 (**2**). The modernist villa that you see here is pleasantly quirky. Although the style is art deco, the architect used a more tempered, regional variant (check out the green roof tiles, which are typically Flemish).

Follow Magdalenastraat until it becomes Marksesteenweg, take a right onto Graaf Karel de Goedelaan, and then walk up the first street on your left, Sint-Martens-Latemlaan. At number 1, you will find the former Magdalena swimming pool (**3**). The pool closed in 2019 and will soon be incorporated in the campus of the Howest University. This masterpiece is a joint effort by several West-Flemish, modernist architects. It is listed as a heritage building, meaning its appearance may not be altered during the building's renovation. Which is a great relief, because this is a functionalist, almost pre-brutalist beauty! The design is groundbreaking, even by today's standards, and was considered very modern at the time because of its adherence to new hygienic standards, which stated that there should be separate circulation routes in the building for shoes vs. no shoes and changing rooms vs. swimming pool. The pool area had glass walls, seamlessly integrating with the green areas that surrounded it. By raising the windows, however, the swimmers still enjoyed privacy. Another novelty was the cafeteria, with a view of the pool, of course.

3. Sint-Martenslatemlaan 1, Paul Felix, Jan Tanghe, Jan De Jaegere, Christian Van der Plaetse (1960)

Continue to walk down Sint-Martens-Latemlaan and you will immediately spot a white bungalow on your right, the first of many in the Skatchkoff neighbourhood. Turn right onto Emiel Clauslaan, then left onto Albijn van Den Abeelelaan, and continue to walk until it turns into Konstant Permekelaan.

In the meantime, feast your eyes on the modernist bungalows around you. The one at number 15 (**4**) is a personal favourite. This area was completely designed by Kortrijk architect Jan De Jaegere, who also collaborated on the design for the Magdalena swimming pool. Originally owned by Jesuit friars, the area was subdivided into plots and assigned to De Jaegere in the 1960s.

4. Skatchkoffwijk (Konstant Permekelaan etc.), Jan De Jaegere (1964)

Follow Konstant Permekelaan around the bend, then turn left onto Sint-Martens-Latemlaan again. Walk back to the pool. Once you're in front of the pool, walk into the park and through it to the other end. Here, you should see a roundabout. Go straight ahead, cross the street, and walk down Burgemeester Felix de Bethunelaan.

Walk under the railway bridge to get to the next roundabout. At the next roundabout, cross the street and continue straight down Burgemeester Felix de Bethunelaan. At the top of this street, turn left onto Aalbeeksesteenweg and then right onto Beverlaaihof. Number 5 (**5**) is an understated example of post-war modernism by Dan Craet (whose work is featured extensively in the Mariakerke tour). The original volume has been preserved, but an annex was added at the front left.

Take a right onto Beverlaai, then left onto Condédreef. Turn left onto Burgemeester Pyckestraat. Once you've passed number 69 on your right, continue walking until you spot a fence to your left. Behind it lies the impressive, early 1960s Verrijzeniskerk (**6**) by André De Smedt. With some luck the gate is open and you'll be able to admire this unique church's impressive interior. But first, some information on the architect(ure). Although it seems to be a completely innovative design, De Smedt was probably inspired by a church in Saint Louis, Missouri, which was built around the same time. De Smedt had travelled to the US shortly before developing this design, and we can assume that he met Gyo Obata, the Japanese architect who created it. Whether or not this is a copy is impossible to determine, but the similarities are glaringly obvious. Either way, the church was and still is a feast for the eyes, with too many details to list. The most striking feature are the magnificent stained-glass windows, which

Verrijzeniskerk, Burgemeester Pyckestraat, André De Smedt (1963)

were recently restored. If you do manage to have a peek inside, then don't forget to have a look at the hallway at the rear, which makes a radical break with the rest of the church in terms of style. The connection between the church and school behind it is conceived as a conservatory, featuring beautiful red and black panelling on the ceiling and free-standing columns. 6. Verrijzeniskerk, Burgemeester Pyckestraat, André De Smedt (1963)

Once you've seen enough of the church, walk back to Burgemeester Pyckestraat and turn left. Take the second street on your right, Sint-Sebastiaanslaan, and walk until it turns into a footpath. Follow the path at the intersection with Loofstraat. At the next intersection, turn left onto Wolvenstraat, and then right onto Jozef Berteelestraat. At the top of the street, turn right onto Doorniksewijk and stop to admire number 187 (**7**). Signed Poly Scherpereel (see the signature above the door), it is suspected that this was the architect's own house, and what a delight it is. The meticulous restoration highlights the many art deco details: the grille on the door, the graphic joinery, the stained-glass windows, and a superb example of cimorné. A material that you will often run into on other routes, cimorné (a portmanteau of "cement" and "ornate") is a typical Belgian façade finishing technique that was invented and patented during the interbellum period. At the end of the 1920s, the Walloon plasterer Pierre Pétroons developed a decorative plaster based on a cement mortar, into which he incorporated waste glass. He was inspired by the Italian terrazzo technique of experimenting with pieces of brightly-coloured opal glass to create textured, colourful surfaces.

7. Doorniksewijk 187, Poly Scherpereel (1930)

Now turn back and walk in the other direction of Doorniksewijk. You'll immediately notice that several other interbellum buildings have been preserved here. Some of these were also designed by Scherpereel, such as the one at number 185, or at number 166, which is not as perfectly preserved.

Keep walking until you pass 136A (**8**), another wonderful example of a design by Scherpereel. The curved second-floor window is particularly striking and the figurative grille on the round window next to the front door is impossible to miss. You'll find the last Scherpereel on this street at number 84 (**9**) and once again it's worth taking a closer look. We can only guess what lies behind these stunning façades. At number 31 (**10**), however, you can walk right in, because part of this bistro's art deco features have been preserved in all their glory. Originally an inn (also named Au Casino), it was redesigned in 1931 by Jan Robert Vanhoenacker for a local brewery called Lust.

8. Doorniksewijk 136A, Werner Van Spranghe (1930s)

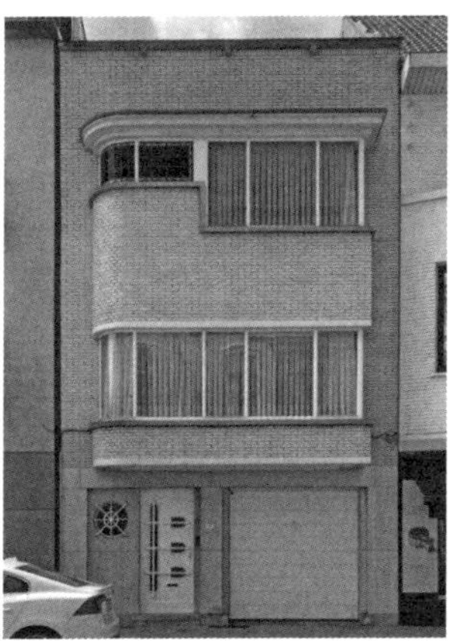

Turn right just past Au Casino onto Kanonstraat, then take a right onto Sint-Denijsestraat. Then turn left onto Filips van de Elzaslaan, and continue to walk down this street until the intersection with Oudenaardsesteenweg. Walk down Oudenaardsesteenweg. Number 5 (**11**) on your left stands out with its gleaming tiles and curved edges. But the most remarkable feature has to be the figurative grille on the door, depicting a nature scene.

Now turn left onto Deken Degryselaan (**12**) or, as it shall henceforth be known, Art Deco Heaven. Take your time to walk down this street as there are too many gems to elaborate on all of them. Pay special attention to numbers 3, 13, 15, 16, 19, and 25!

12. Deken Degryselaan 3, 19, 16

Next, turn left onto Elfde-julilaan, left again onto Graaf Boudewijn IX-laan, then right onto Tuighuisstraat, and then left onto Rijkswachtstraat, bringing you to your last stop, the large building at number 5 (**13**). The former home of Kortrijk's fire brigade is currently being repurposed to house a public sharing platform. Given that so many modernist buildings met with a tragic fate – they are demolished or irreparably “renovated” – admiring this building seems like a good way to end this tour. It’s the way forward: a meticulous restoration, after which the building is put to good use. Here’s hoping that we’ll see (much) more of this in the future.

To return to the train station, take the next street on your left, Sint-Antoniusstraat, and then turn right onto Zwevegemsestraat. You’ll arrive at a roundabout. Turn right towards the bridge, walk under it, and then immediately turn left onto Spoorweglaan, which takes you right back to the station.

Eeklo

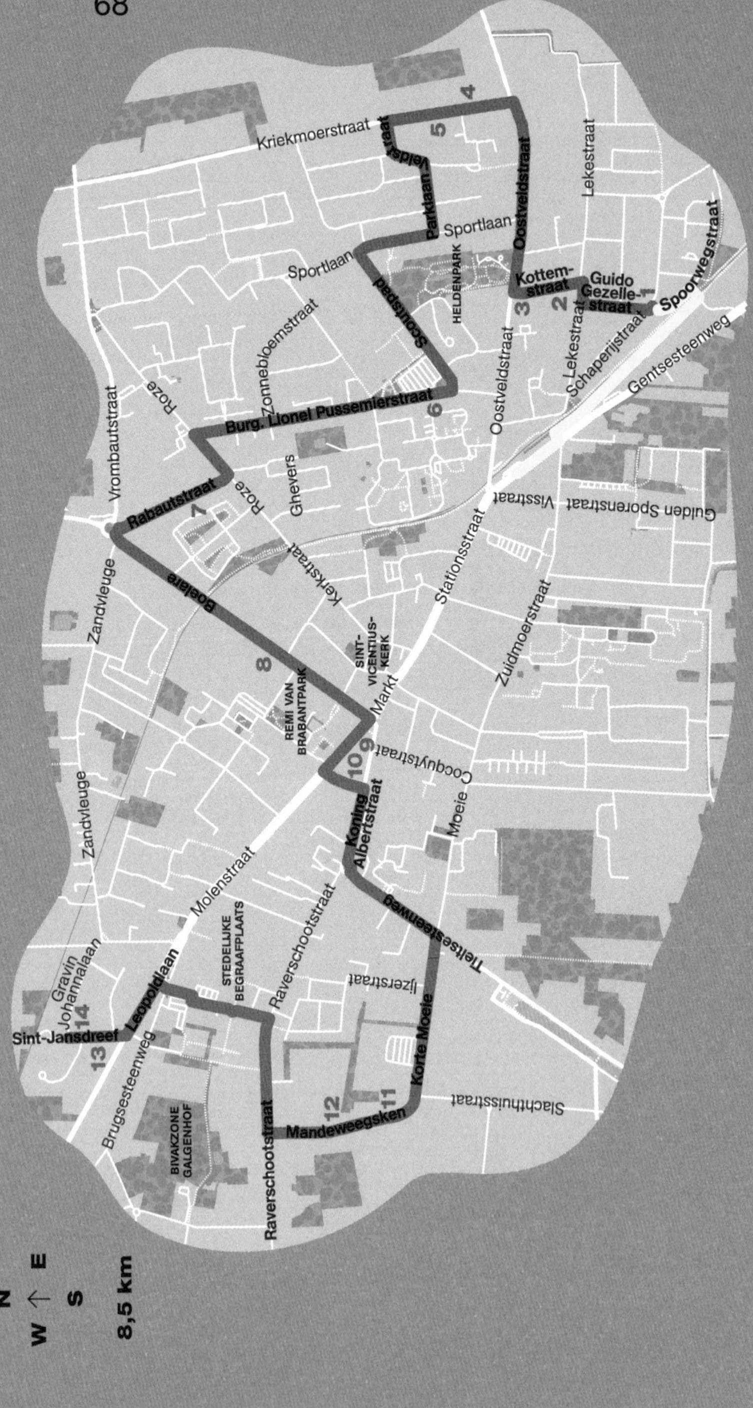
Kriekmoerstraat
Veldstraat
Parklaan
Sportlaan
Sportlaan
Oostveldstraat
Lekestraat
HELDENPARK
Scoutspad
Kottem-
straat
Guido
Gezelle-
straat
Spoorwegstraat
Lekestraat
Schaperijstraat
Gentsesteenweg
Oostveldstraat
Zonnebloemstraat
Roze
Burg. Lionel Pussemierstraat
Vrombautstraat
Ghevers
Roze
Rabautstraat
Visstraat
Guldn Sporenstraat
Stationsstraat
Kerkstraat
Zandvleuge
Boelare
SINT-
VICENTIUS-
KERK
Zuidmoerstraat
Markt
REMI VAN
BRABANTPARK
Cocquytstraat
Zandvleuge
Koning
Albertstraat
Moeie
Molenstraat
Raverschootstraat
STEDELIJKE
BEGRAAFPLAATS
Tieltsesteenweg
Gravin
Johannalaan
Leopoldlaan
Ijzerstraat
Sint-Jansdreef
Brugsesteenweg
Korte Moeie
Slachthuisstraat
BIVAKZONE
GALGENHOF
Raverschootstraat
Mandeweegsken
1
2
3
4
5
6
7
8
9
10
11
12
13
14
N
W E
S
8,5 km

1 Guido Gezellestraat
Louis Geirnaert & Paul Bekaert
1964

2 Kottemstraat 10
Louis Geirnaert
1957

3 Oostveldstraat 83B
Lode Aerts, Jozef De Coninck & Frans Vandendael
1965

4 Kriekmoerstraat 119
Marc Van Cleven
1966

5 Kriekmoerstraat 120
Louis Geirnaert
1962

6 Burgemeester Lionel Pussemierstraat 166
Louis Geirnaert
1965

7 Rabautstraat 66
Marc Dessauvage
1962

8 Boelare 79
Alexander Meuleman
1933

9 Molenstraat 1
Alexander Meuleman
1932

10 Molenstraat 33
Alexander Meuleman
1939

11 Mandeweegsken 73
Louis Geirnaert
1959

12 Mandeweegsken 54
Louis Geirnaert
1961

13 Leopoldlaan 30
François Langeraert
1937

14 Sint-Jansdreef 10
Louis Geirnaert
1957

Of all the locations in this book, Eeklo is probably the underdog. It's not a big city, nor is it particularly known for its architecture or heritage. Like Ghent and Kortrijk, Eeklo was once a thriving town, thanks to its involvement in the textile industry. Industry generates prosperity, and some of the art deco gems that you can still see in the city today formerly belonged to wealthy industrialist families.

But wealth and its ties with fabulous houses aside, it's the creations of one Eeklo native in particular that make the city worthy of architectural scrutiny: the buildings of Louis Geirnaert, one of the unsung pioneers of post-war modernist architecture who mainly worked in the 1950s and 60s. He designed more than half of the stops on this route and hopefully this chapter is another step towards wider recognition and appreciation of his work.

Since this walking tour is not a loop and the stops are slightly farther apart, you should perhaps consider adding a bicycle to your adventure pack. If you do prefer to walk, keep in mind that once you've reached the end of the tour, you'll have to walk all the way back. But hey, all of these buildings are so stunning that it's a real pleasure to see them twice!

With your back to the main entrance of the train station, take a left and walk past the car park. Turn left again, and walk along the railway tracks. Continue to follow the tracks until you reach Oude Gentweg, where you turn left and cross the tracks, and then immediately take a left again onto Spoorwegstraat. Walk all the way to the end of the street to get to your first stop, a social housing development designed by – yes, you guessed it! – Louis Geirnaert (**1**). Turn left onto Schaperijstraat, and then right onto Guido Gezellestraat. It's like stepping back in time – and look at those vibrant colours! Thankfully these dwellings, which were completed in 1964, were renovated in 2016 and their exteriors restored to their former glory. In the 1960s, most social housing was not this modern, but these houses have flat roofs and colourful panelling, as well as warm air heating, which was considered quite revolutionary in those days.

1. Guido Gezellestraat, Louis Geirnaert & Paul Bekaert (1964)

The cheerful combination of shapes and colours that you see here is a first taste of Geirnaert's talent and skill. Born (in 1930) and raised in Eeklo, Geirnaert was the second child of Richard Geirnaert and his second wife (his first wife died at a tragically young age). After studying architecture in Ghent, Geirnaert started his own practice back home at the age of 24. Fortunately, Eeklo was a rapidly growing town in the 1950s, and the need for new housing provided him with lots of opportunities to develop and establish his vision. As Geirnaert's ideas were often deemed too modern or too radical, some clients were reticent about giving him carte blanche. Some people even questioned who on earth would want to live in a bunker. But as you will see, those houses for which he was given free rein stand out the most. Enough talking, let's go check out some of his designs!

At the end of Guido Gezellestraat, take a right onto Lekestraat, and then a left onto Kottemstraat where you stop at number 10 (**2**) to admire another playful façade by Geirnaert. His designs weren't just fun, they were also practical and clever, revolving around his clients and their way of living. This house was designed for a paediatrician who had his practice on the ground floor. To make his patients feel more at ease, he asked Geirnaert to design a playroom instead of a waiting room. In addition, the consultation table was designed in such a way that children could climb on it themselves. Sliding walls ensured that the laboratory, office, and consultation room could be separated from each other when necessary. 2. Kottemstraat 10, Louis Geirnaert (1957)

Continue your tour by walking to the end of Kottemstraat. On the corner with Oostveldstraat you can spot the modern Church of Our Lady (**3**). While this striking building looks quite minimalist at first glance, it features some unique characteristics that still make it stand out today: a separate bell tower, doors with beautiful lettering, monumental stained-glass windows, and massive wooden beams inside. Do peek inside if the door happens to be open, so you can admire it in all its glory.

Now turn right onto Oostveldstraat and take the second street on your left, Kriekmoerstraat. Have a look at number 119 on your right (**4**) for a more toned-down version of post-war modernism. This bungalow by Marc Van Cleven is less playful and much more functionalist than the houses you've seen so far. Unfortunately, that's all the information

Church of Our Lady, Oostveldstraat 83B,
Lode Aerts, Jozef De Coninck & Frans Vandendael (1965)

that we have, but the façade definitely fuels the imagination so feel free to dream up the rest!

4. Kriekmoerstraat 119, Marc Van Cleven (1966)

Just down the road, at number 120 (**5**), it's back to our main man, Mr Geirnaert. The clients for these two semi-detached houses were two families, who knew each other and who wanted a modern residence. As they liked Geirnaert's style, they decided to commission a house from him. Although both houses look exactly the same, the difference lies in the tiny, practical details. Because one faces northwards and the other southwards, Geirnaert changed the size of the windows and the protruding walls. As the families were close (in every sense of the word), the architect also came up with some economical solutions, such as a shared boiler. With the boiler came an opening (with a door) between the two houses, which allowed them to enter each other's homes. Rather than take issue with it, the owners felt that this had nothing but benefits. When they were babysitting each other's children, for example, they could easily walk into the other house and check in on them. The architect also made sure that his design reflected his clients' personalities. The residents on the left were passionate about music so their banister is shaped like a musical staff, in Geirnaert's beloved primary colours. Over time, one of the families moved out and some changes were made to the house on the right, including on the façade.

5. Kriekmoerstraat 120, Louis Geirnaert (1962)

Walk up the street and take a left onto Veldstraat, which you keep following as it turns left. Then take the second street on your right, which is called Parklaan. On Parklaan, take the third street on your right, Sportlaan. Finally, on Sportlaan, take the first street on your left, Scoutspad, and follow it until the end, where you take a right onto Burgemeester Lionel Pussemierstraat. Number 166 (**6**) is another (ha!) Louis Geirnaert design. Given that this is a terraced house, Geirnaert took a more minimalist approach out of necessity. He designed it late in his career for a friend of one of the owners of the aforementioned semi-detached houses.

Walk to the end of Burgemeester Lionel Pussemierstraat, then turn left on Roze. Take the first street on your right, Rabautstraat, and stop to admire number 66 (**7**). Though it's somewhat similar to the last house (especially in the use of colours), this was not designed by Geirnaert, but by Marc Dessauvage. This architect is particularly known for his brutalist style and for the way in which he revolutionised religious architecture in the 1960s and 1970s. However, Dessauvage also designed private homes. In fact, he is mostly known for the creation of detached houses, paying special attention to their integration into the surrounding landscape, which forms an integral part of the design. In that sense, this terraced house is quite exceptional.

After all this mid-century modernism, the time has come to travel a little further back in time. Continue to walk down Rabautstraat until you reach the roundabout, then take the first street on your left, Vrombautstraat, which first turns into Blommekens and then Boelare. Once you've crossed the railway tracks, you'll notice that many of the buildings that line the street date from the interbellum period. Unfortunately, almost all of them were heavily altered or even destroyed during the war. Fortunately, there are some exceptions to this evolution, and number 79 (**8**) is definitely the best example. As mentioned in the introduction, the sudden emergence of modernist houses in Eeklo was linked to the presence of wealthy textile industrialists, and this house illustrates just that. Alexander Meuleman hailed from Ghent and designed houses in a distinctive art deco style, before moving on to New Objectivity later in his career. This example obviously dates from his art deco period and features some stunning details, as you can see on the newly restored façade. The alternating brickwork is an obvious nod to the Amsterdam School, while the grille on the door and the stained-glass window above it are typical art deco elements. The interaction between the different coloured bricks and black joinery is simply magnificent. Inside, the original lay-out has been preserved and the original stairwell is still an absolute eye-catcher ninety years later.

8. Boelare 79, Alexander Meuleman (1933)

Follow Boelare until the intersection, then turn right on Molenstraat and look to your left to find restaurant Bistro d'O (**9**) on the corner of the street, also by Alexander Meuleman. While the ground floor has been renovated, the top floor has been preserved in its original state (although initially the façade remained unpainted). This also has some interesting brickwork.

Turn right to see even more work by Meuleman at number 33 (**10**). This stately home, which he designed for a bicycle manufacturer, has undergone no alterations whatsoever. This original art deco gem is a fine example of the Streamline Moderne substyle, which derives its name from the similarities that this style of architecture shares with the designs of old-time ocean liners. Eeklo is nowhere near the sea, but you can almost smell it here. Notice the streamlined, rounded shapes, the tubular railing that is very similar to that of a ship, the higher brick side walls, and the metal windows. There are some beautiful porthole windows inside. These neat nautical features aren't the only things that make this boat float, however: the house also features intricate stained-glass windows (both on the façade and in the interior), a stunning stairwell, original hardwood and tiled floors, and more. But the real showstopper is the bathroom, featuring marbrite everywhere you look. This obsolete material is a type of opal glass that was coloured with metal oxides to make it look like marble. It was invented by the Belgian Arthur Brancart and produced by his

Molenstraat 33, Alexander Meuleman (1932)

glassware factory in Fauquez. After its presentation at the 1925 International Exhibition of Modern Decorative and Industrial Arts in Paris, it became the factory's flagship product. As such, it was incorporated in many an art deco interior, primarily in bathrooms.

10. Molenstraat 33, Alexander Meuleman (1932)

Now take the next street on your left, René Vermaststraat, then turn right onto Koning Albertstraat. At the roundabout, take the first street on your left, Tieltsesteenweg, and then the first one on your right, Korte Moeie, which turns into Mandeweegsken around the bend. Number 73 (**11**) is another obvious Geirnaert design, but unfortunately the joinery is no longer original. Check out the juxtaposition of materials, the playful volumes, the sculpture on the façade, and that Expo 58 style railing.

11. Mandeweegsken 73, Louis Geirnaert (1959)

Continue to walk down Mandeweegsken and have a look at number 54 on your left (**12**). This modest block of flats was also designed by Geirnaert. The blue Gasal panels and the original typo on the façade, spelling out the residence's name "Kayana", are especially striking.

12. Mandeweegsken 54, Louis Geirnaert (1961)

Next, turn right onto Raverschootstraat, then left onto Kerkhofweg and continue walking until Brugsesteenweg, which you cross to get to Leopoldlaan. In Leopoldlaan, walk to number 30 (**13**) to see some classic art deco. While not nearly as radical as the house you walked past earlier on Molenstraat, this is nonetheless a fine example of interbellum architecture.

With your back to the house, turn left onto Sint-Jansdreef, where you will find Geirnaert's own home (**14**) at number 10. In 1954, several Eeklo creatives joined forces to open the Molenhuis gallery, where they could present their work. With designs on display ranging from architecture and furniture to ceramics and jewellery, Geirnaert's first contribution was a design for student housing. This pop-up gallery avant la lettre proved a tremendous success, attracting six thousand visitors over a three-day period. Among them was Ernella De Roo, who fell for the charms of a passionate Geirnaert as she was led around the gallery. They married a year and a half later. While looking for a place to build their love nest, they bought this plot in 1957. This offered Geirnaert just the opportunity he was looking for to go all out. He decided to follow his every whim, and just look at the superb result! Although the house has undergone some alterations, the spirit of Geirnaert's design is still very much alive. The sculpture on the wall, by the ceramicist Bart Maréchal, has been recently restored and is a testament to Geirnaert's vision

Sint-Jansdreef 10, Louis Geirnaert (1957)

on the harmony between art and architecture. Other modern additions include the façade with panels in diverse colours, the split levels, different types of floors in every room, and the open-plan kitchen.

14. Sint-Jansdreef 10, Louis Geirnaert (1957)

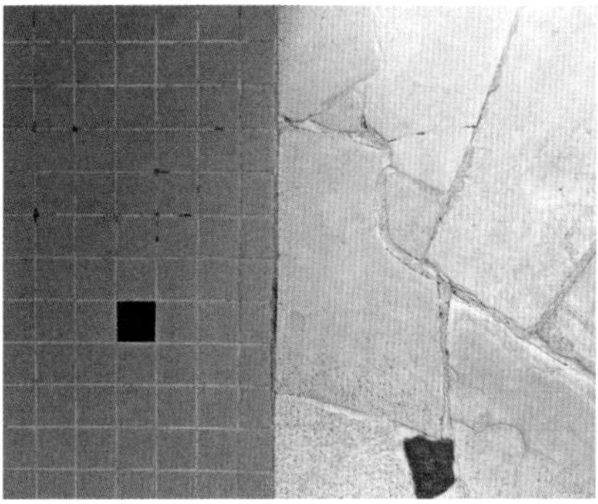

Louis Geirnaert's own home seems like a good end to your walking tour in Eeklo. Here's hoping that it will rekindle interest in this visionary architect and his joyful creations!

Uccle

Rue Jean-Baptiste Colyns
Rue Alphonse Renard
Rue Camille Lemonnier
Rue Jules Lejeune
Avenue Molière
Avenue Molière
Rue Mignot Delstanche
Rue Edmond Picard
Rue Franz Merjay
Avenue Brugmann
Rue Jean-Baptiste Meunier
Rue Joseph Stallaert
Rue Vanderkindere
Rue Vanderkindere
Rue Marie Depage
Rue Edith Cavell
Rue Général Lotz
Rue Gabrielle
Rue Dodonée
Avenue Winston Churchill
Avenue Winston Churchill
Rue Ernest Gossart
Avenue Montjoie
Rue Edith Cavell
PARC MONTJOIE
PARC BRUGMANN
Avenue Adolphe Dupuich
Avenue Léo Errera
Avenue Montjoie
Avenue Moscicki
Rue Edith Cavell
Avenue Brunard
Bosveldweg
Rue Roberts Jones
Rue Edith Cavell
Rue Langeveld
Avenue de Sumatra
Avenue du Hoef
Rue Zeecrabbe
Avenue De Fré
1
2
3
4
5
6
7
8
9
10
11
12
13
14

N

W ↑ E

S

3,5 km

1 Avenue Molière 208
Joe Raemaekers
1928

2 Rue Alphonse Renard 60
Henry van de Velde
1929

3 Rue Camille Lemonnier 112
Robert Puttemans
1929

4 Rue Jules Lejeune 69
Paul-Amaury Michel
1935

5 Rue Général Lotz 69
Simone Guillissen-Hoa
1955

6 Rue Ernest Gossart 34
Louis Tenaerts
1936

7 Avenue Montjoie 127
Stanislas Jasinski
1935

8 Avenue Brunard 41
Jacques Wybauw
1960

9 Rue Edith Cavell 119
Raphaël Delville
1933

10 Avenue Léo Errera 41
Léon Govaerts & Alexis Van Vaerenbergh
1928

11 Avenue Léo Errera 63
Jean Dumont
1950

12 Rue Langeveld 21
Simone Guillissen-Hoa
1965

13 Rue Langeveld 46
Robert Puttemans
1958

14 Avenue de Sumatra 8
Jacques Dupuis
1954

Affluent residential Uccle, which is located in the south of Brussels, has a rich architectural history, with art nouveau, art deco, and modernism co-existing harmoniously. One of the city's greenest areas, it borders on La Cambre forest, which is home to the prestigious, progressive art school of the same name, where many of the architects that are included in this walking tour once studied. So you won't be surprised to hear that many of them decided to build a home of their own in this area.

The walk begins with two buildings that are technically in the neighbouring district of Ixelles, but close enough to Uccle that they are worth including.

After getting off at the tram at Molière, walk towards Avenue Molière to number 208 (**1**) – an eight-storey block of flats by the little-known architect Joe Ramaekers. Dating from 1928, the design of this hidden gem with its intricate brickwork and original typographic signage was clearly influenced by the Amsterdam School. Unfortunately, we have no idea what the apartments look like on the inside, but behind the door to the left of the main entrance lies an office, the corridor of which alone is worth seeing. Besides a mosaic floor with a colourful pattern, it also features a beautiful wall sculpture by Oscar De Clerck.

1. Avenue Molière 208, Joe Raemaekers (1928)

Continue walking down the road and turn left onto Rue Alphonse Renard. At number 60 you'll find Maison Wolfers (**2**), designed by Henry van de Velde, the founder of the La Cambre art school. This townhouse from 1929 is a good example of the reductive design language in the architect's later work. The garden was designed by Lucien

Boucher. Van de Velde designed the house for a manufacturer called Wolfers and his family. They were obviously well-off and enjoyed a pre-war bourgeois lifestyle. The house was designed to be – only – enjoyed by the family. Their live-in servants had separate quarters and took care of all the manual labour, such as cooking and cleaning. Fast forward to the 1970s, by which time this had become an archaic mode of living, rendering the house impractical. It was deemed more of a monument than a liveable space. But this was exactly what its last owner, Herman Daled, who lived here until his death in 2020, liked about the house. Daled wasn't just passionate about art (he was the founder of Wiels, among others), he was also an avid art collector. And that's exactly how he treated the house: as a work of art that should be preserved. When he purchased it, it was largely intact. In those instances where restorations were undertaken over the years, they were not designed to bring the house up to modern standards, but to restore it to its original state. From a modern perspective, this makes for a house that is quite impractical. The kitchen, for example, is in the cellar, as this is where the servants used to cook. Now that this gigantic townhouse has lost its custodian, it's unclear what will happen to it. Luckily, it has since been listed as a monument.

Turn right onto Rue Jean-Baptiste Colyns and then right again on Rue Camille Lemonnier. At number 112 (**3**), you'll find a three-storey house in the rationalist style, which Robert Puttemans designed for himself in 1929. It features typically Belgian yellow brick with contrasting green window frames.

3. Rue Camille Lemonnier 112, Robert Puttemans (1929)

Continuing ahead, at the roundabout take the first street on your left onto Rue Jules Lejeune. At number 69 you will find the incredibly well-preserved Maison de Verre (**4**), named after the iconic 1929 Parisian building by Pierre Chareau. The house was designed in 1935 by Paul-Amaury Michel and – with its pilotis, roof garden, horizontal windows, and open plan – is clearly influenced by Le Corbusier's 'The Five Points of a New Architecture'.

4. Rue Jules Lejeune 69, Paul-Amaury Michel (1935)

Walk back to the roundabout, crossing it onto Rue de l'Anémone. Continue walking to Rue Marie Depage, then turn left onto Rue Général Lotz. Number 69 (**5**) is an understated house with a white rendered rhythmic façade and contrasting black brick, which was designed by Simone Guillissen-Hoa. Born in Beijing in 1916, she was only the second woman architect to graduate from La Cambre (in 1938). Guillissen-Hoa later collaborated with the pioneering architect Jacques Dupuis and, from 1939 to 1946, was also an employee at

Alfred Roth's Swiss architecture studio. Recently the house's interior was completely renovated, and a third floor added. Unfortunately, this intervention detracts from the original design. Thankfully, the outlook of the original façade has been preserved.

At the end of Rue Général Lotz, turn left onto Avenue Winston Churchill, then take the second street on your right, Rue Ernest Gossart. The house at number 34 (**6**), with its curved façade and port-hole windows, is a prime example of the Streamline Moderne style. It was designed by an architect called Louis Tenaerts in 1936 for the painter Raoul Labarre. At the end of his career, in the early 1990s, Tenaerts claimed that he had designed 1,635 buildings, making him the most prolific architect among his peers. His career spanned five decades, and he switched effortlessly from one style to the other, in accordance with his clients' tastes. But he excelled in the Streamline Moderne style.

6. Rue Ernest Gossart 34, Louis Tenaerts (1936)

At the intersection of Rue Ernest Gossart and Avenue Montjoie, at number 127 (**7**), you will find a block of flats by Stanislas Jasinski, a self-taught architect who worked for Victor Horta and Henry van de Velde. A keen traveller, he met Robert Mallet-Stevens and Le Corbusier in France. The latter especially made a lasting impression on Jasinski. A trip to New York in the 1930s, with its modern high-rises, inspired Jasinski to question the archaic construction techniques that were still being used in Europe. He built this block of flats, which dates from 1935, upon his return from the United States. It is one of the first examples of what he called "modular building". Jasinski's vision was initially radical and often relegated to paper, precisely because it was so radical. Over time, he found support and a sounding board for his ideas, however, among his peers. He often published articles on architecture in the influential *7 Arts* artists' journal, an initiative of the architect Victor Bourgeois and his brother, the poet Pierre Bourgeois. The co-founders of *7 Arts* were artists Pierre-Louis Flouquet and Karel Maes, and composer Georges Monnier, who were joined by numerous other creatives, including René Magritte, Victor Servranckx, Marcel-Louis Baugniet, Huib Hoste, and Jozef Peeters. The journal quickly became an important platform for the promotion of modernity in Belgium and Europe. The articles, manifestos, and reviews in it were intended to "revolutionise, without hierarchy, the links between architecture, town planning, literature, cinema, the decorative arts, music, and theatre, and to report on literary and artistic news both in Belgium and in Europe". The magazine had a lasting influence, establishing connections between progressive artists and architects all over Europe.

7. Avenue Montjoie 127, Stanislas Jasinski (1935)

With your back to the building, turn right onto Avenue Montjoie, then left on Avenue Brunard. At number 41 (**8**), you'll see a house in the functionalist style by the architect Jacques Wybauw, which he designed in 1960 for himself. Despite the fact that this is a simple cube-shaped building, details such as the contrasting colours of the brickwork and the irregular positioning of the windows add interest. At the rear, facing south, the house opens up entirely onto the garden. The positioning on a sloping site led Wybauw to organise the space in staggered levels: the rooms at ground level, which look out onto the avenue and are west-facing, are situated one flight of steps below the other living spaces. From the outside, you can deduce this organisation from the discreet staggering of windows.

8. Avenue Brunard 41, Jacques Wybauw (1960)

Continue walking along Avenue Brunard until you reach Rue Edith Cavell. In front of you, at number 119 (**9**), you'll see what is possibly one of the smallest modernist buildings ever built. This tiny white house with curved balconies was designed by Raphaël Delville in 1933, and his name can still be seen on the building's façade.

9. Rue Edith Cavell 119, Raphaël Delville (1933)

Next, turn left onto Rue Edith Cavell, then right onto Rue Roberts Jones and then right again onto Avenue Léo Errera. Number 41 (**10**) is the former home of art collectors Alice and David Van Buuren, which David designed himself, and which was built by Léon Govaerts and Alexis Van Vaerenbergh in 1928. Unlike David, Alice came from humble origins, and David vowed to introduce her to the world of arts and culture that was so dear to him. Almost everything in their house was made to measure by craftsmen and artists, from the carpets and the furniture to the lighting and everything in between. David later became the director of a private bank and amassed a fortune, which he largely spent on their magnificent art collection. Although they were quite reclusive, they engaged with the artists whom they collected. They became the patrons of Gustave Van de Woestyne, whose work can still be seen inside the house. To give you an idea of just how wealthy the Van Buurens were: when the war broke out in 1940, the couple moved their art collection to safety and fled to New York, where they lived in a suite at the Plaza Hotel for five years. Fortunately, the house was still standing upon their return.

10. Avenue Léo Errera 41, Léon Govaerts & Alexis Van Vaerenbergh (1928)

Avenue Léo Errera 41, Léon Govaerts & Alexis Van Vaerenbergh (1928)

Avenue Léo Errera 41, Léon Govaerts & Alexis Van Vaerenbergh (1928)

Per Alice's wish, the building is now a museum, showcasing the couple's remarkable collection of furniture and modern art in the original art deco interior.

As you exit the museum, retrace your steps and walk right until number 63, where you will find the architect Jean Dumont's own home (**11**), in a typical 1950s style. White brick walls have been combined with natural stone and alternating brick-work on the left side, making for a dynamic façade. It's obvious Dumont was inspired or influenced by Jacques Dupuis' masterpiece Le Parador, which was built a few years earlier and also combines modern and classical elements. The comparison is most obvious in the door, with its star motif and the columns that flank it.

11. Avenue Léo Errera 63, Jean Dumont (1950)

Continue walking, then turn left onto Rue Roberts Jones again. Turn right onto Rue Edith Cavell, and then left onto Rue Langeveld. At number 21 (**12**), you'll find another building by Guillissen-Hoa, a small block of flats with clean lines and large windows, which she designed in 1965. The flats – the architect lived in one of them herself – are incredibly spacious and light. Guillissen-Hoa's flat, which is now occupied by her son, has been preserved in its original state. 12. Rue Langeveld 21, Simone Guillissen-Hoa (1965)

Further along the same street, at number 46 (**13**), you can see another house that Robert Puttemans designed for his family in 1958. Puttemans built this bungalow-like structure almost thirty years after his first residence on Avenue Camille Lemonnier, and it's fascinating to see the evolution in his style. Recently, the original façade, which was in a dire state, was completely renovated to bring it up to modern-day standards. It's darker in colour now, but thankfully its original spirit has been preserved.

Opposite the Puttemans house you'll find Avenue de Sumatra. At number 8 you can see a superb building by Jacques Dupuis, your last stop. Designed in 1954 for the art collector Madeleine Everaert, Maison Everaert (**14**), with its sculptural canopy over the front door, features the architect's most iconic façade. Dupuis' use of organic shapes meant that his design lacked right angles, with many of his buildings looking downright progressive as a result. Legend has it that the enigmatic and hedonistic architect, who loved to party, lost an eye while popping open a bottle of champagne. This dwelling comprises two flats: the owner lived on the ground floor, renting out the upper floor. From the street it appears closed off, but in true modernist fashion, it opens up at the rear, with great views of the garden. 14. Avenue de Sumatra 8, Jacques Dupuis (1954)

To return to the nearest tram stop, walk back to Avenue Winston Churchill via Rue Edith Cavell.

Ostend

STATION OOSTENDE
Brandariskaai
Natiënkaai
Vissers-kaai
Leopold III-laan
Vindictivelaan
Jozef II-straat
JACHTHAVEN MERCATOR
Christinastraat
MARIA HENDRIKAPARK
Verenigde Natieslaan
Euphrosina Beernaertstraat
DE GROTE POST
Leopold II-laan
LEOPOLDPARK
Alfons Pieterslaan
Romestraat
Kaaistraat
Edith Cavellstraat
BOTERPUT
Adolf Buylstraat
Langestraat
Marie-Joséplein
Leon Spilliaertstraat
SINT-JOZEFSKERK
KURSAAL
Van Iseghemlaan
Karel Janssenslaan
Rogierlaan
Jules Peurquaetstraat
Peter Benoitstraat
KONINKLIJKE STALLINGEN
Koninginnelaan
Prinsenlaan
Leffingestraat
Tarwe-straat
Plantenstraat
Frère-Orbanstraat
Hennepstraat
Albert I-promenade
Koningstraat
Warschaustraat
Torhoutsesteenweg
Nieuwpoortsesteenweg
Velodroomstraat
HEILIG HART-KERK
Nijverheidstraat
JAPANSE TUIN
Wellingtonstraat
Koningin Astridlaan
Koning Boudewijnpromenade
Sportstraat
NOORDZEE
KONINKLIJKE GAANDERIJEN
WELLINGTON PAARDENRENBAAN
Zeedijk
1
2
3
4
5
6
7
8
9
10
11
12
13
14
15
16
17
18
19
20
21
22
23
N
W
E
S
4,5 km

1 Madridstraat 5
Alfred Danneel
1930s

2 Marie-Joséplein 3
Joseph Vanderbanck
1928

3 Monaco-Plein
Léon Stynen
1950

4 Koningsstraat 43A
Paul Felix
1959

5 Warschaustraat 12
Bernard Christiaens
1937

6 Warschaustraat 14-20
unknown
1930s

7 Warschaustraat 22
Albert-Victor Fobert
1938

8 Velodroomstraat 11
Silvain Smis
1930s

9 Eduard de Cuyperstraat 11A
Silvain Smis
1933

10 Heilig-Hartlaan 21
Maurice-Albert Hautekiet
1930s

11 Heilig-Hartplein 7
Silvain Smis
1930s

12 Heilig-Hartplein 8
Silvain Smis
1930s

13 Nijverheidstraat 36
G. Galle
1930s

14 Nijverheidstraat 42
Jerome Brackx
1930s

15 Plantenstraat 92
unknown
1930s

16 Plantenstraat 78
Marcel Van Coillie
1930s

17 Plantenstraat 55, 49
unknown
1930s

18 Frère-Orbanstraat 65
Marcel Van Coillie
1933

19 Prinsenlaan
1930s

20 Gentstraat 6
Gaston Eysselinck
1950

21 Romestraat 11
Gaston Eysselinck
1955

22 Euphrosina Beernaertstraat 21B
Jan Tanghe
1957

23 Euphrosina Beernaertstraat 21A
Bernard Christiaens
1937

Upon your arrival by train in Ostend, it is immediately apparent why this city is called the queen of seaside resorts in Belgium: how can you fail to marvel at the railway station's grandeur and old-time glory? That same grandeur, which extends throughout the city centre, is a legacy of Belgium's (horrendous) colonial past.

Although rundown and somewhat rough around the edges at times, many modernist gems have fortunately been preserved since the 1930s (or 40s, 50s and 60s). In Ostend, you're always only a short walk away from the next remarkable building. This walking tour is therefore simply based on maximum concentration and availability. The selected area is not too far out of the centre, with lots of modernist dwellings in close proximity. It also showcases a side of Ostend that is all too often overlooked: the beautiful residential dwellings on the town's fringe.

Get off the tram at Marie-Joséplein, and walk towards Madridstraat where you stop at number 5, a beautifully maintained interbellum block of flats by Alfred Danneel with retail spaces on the ground floor level (**1**). The wavy façade is reminiscent of the sea, adding an element of poetry to the design.

1. Madridstraat 5, Alfred Danneel (1930s)

Turn back and take a right on Marie-Joséplein and continue walking straight ahead. You'll pass the grand art deco hotel/restaurant Hotel Du Parc on your right (**2**), after which another iconic feature of Ostend's skyline awaits you just around the corner: the Casino Kursaal by Léon Stynen (**3**). Chances are that you walked past this casino many times as you took a stroll down the promenade, but very few people know what lies behind the monumental windows that face the sea. The interior is nothing short of wonderful: from the glamorous lobby and the former lounge with sculptures by Pierre Caille to the grand theatre with a direct view of the sea – there's so much to discover. The casino is privately owned and has been revamped over the years, but the event space has remained completely intact thanks to meticulous restorations over the years.

Casino Kursaal, Monaco-Plein, painting by Edgard Tytgat

One of the more recent efforts consisted of the restoration of a giant fresco by Paul Delvaux, which had become yellowed due to nicotine. Stynen's design was radically modern: the use of reinforced concrete for the building's skeleton, monumental windows with slim aluminium frames, and the magnificent combination of architecture and art by employing artists to create in situ artworks – it's all there and it's every bit as jaw-dropping as it was in 1953.

3. Casino Kursaal, Monaco-Plein, Léon Stynen (1950), ceramics by Pierre Caille

Casino Kursaal, Monaco-Plein, artwork by Julien Van Vlasselaer

Casino Kursaal, Monaco-Plein, fresco by Paul Delvaux

Turn back and take a right at Koningsstraat where you can find the former home and office of legendary Ostend architect Paul Felix at number 43A (**4**). The block of flats was commissioned by private clients in the 1950s, but Felix reserved the top floor for himself and became a co-owner of the building. Both the exterior and the interior are very functional and light, although the placement of the terraces adds rhythm to the building's façade.

4. Koningsstraat 43A, Paul Felix (1959)

Take the next street on your left, Kemmelbergstraat, and the first street on your right at the roundabout, Warschaustraat, where you can discover a row of remarkable buildings. Number 12 (**5**) is a lovely example of the New Objectivity style by Bernard Christiaens, where time seems to have stood still. The combination of different materials such as tiles, brick, marbrite and granite on the façade stands out in particular. And then there's the stunning original lettering that spells out the residence's name.

5. Warschaustraat 12, Bernard Christiaens (1937)

The design of numbers 14 through 20 (**6**) is in a similar vein: simple, stripped-down art deco. Unfortunately, many of the original features have been altered over the years and the architects are unknown.

6. Warschaustraat 16, unknown (1930s)

Number 22 (**7**), by Albert-Victor Fobert, is in mint condition, however. The remaining grille on the door and the lettering are especially worthy of your attention.

7. Warschaustraat 22, Albert-Victor Fobert (1938)

Continue walking down Warschaustraat, turning right at Wellingtonstraat, and then taking the third street on your left, Koninginnelaan. Turn right onto Velodroomstraat, where at number 11 (**8**) you can see the first house by Silvain Smis, who will feature heavily in the rest of this tour. Smis was born and raised in Ostend and designed various modernist buildings in the city. He was not afraid to use colour and his façades combine a diverse range of materials with an aesthetic sensibility.

Continue walking down Velodroomstraat, which turns into Eduard De Cuyperstraat, until you reach number 11A (**9**), which just so happens to be Smis's own home. The façade is both more refined and grander than that of other houses in Ostend which he designed; the sculptures by Daniël Devriendt add an almost regal touch. The current owner is carefully restoring the house to its former glory and the façade work was recently completed, so enjoy the gleaming tiles and the sandblasted brick. 9. Eduard de Cuyperstraat 11A, Silvain Smis (1933)

Now walk on to Heilig-Hartlaan, where you can spot several interbellum façades. Number 21 (**10**), by Maurice-Albert Hautekiet, is especially noteworthy, as it was lovingly restored and features interesting brickwork and art deco details such as the tiling around the door.

On Heilig-Hartplein, look to your right for number 7 (**11**) and then to your left for number 8 (**12**), two fine examples of Smis's signature style. These buildings were designed by the same architect, but were also both located in a corner of the square, resulting in two truly remarkable façades.

11. Heilig-Hartplein 7, Silvain Smis (1930s)

12. Heilig-Hartplein 8, Silvain Smis (1930s)

Turn left onto Professor Mac Leodstraat and then take a sharp right onto Nijverheidstraat. Unfortunately, the joinery of number 36 (**13**), a design by G. Galle, has been renewed, but some of the playful art deco elements have been preserved. At number 42 (**14**) you'll find a similar house, by Jerome Brackx.

Turn left onto Karel van de Woestijnestraat, cross the road at Torhoutsesteenweg and walk down Hennepstraat, then immediately take a left onto Plantenstraat. On the corner, at number 92 (**15**), you can see a wonderful (albeit anonymous) example of the New Objectivity style, bordering on the Streamline Moderne. Unfortunately, as has often been the case on this route, the original door was replaced by a modern one.

15. Plantenstraat 92, unknown (1930s)

Plantenstraat ("Plant Street") doesn't just have a beautiful name, it is also lined with several architectural gems. Number 78 (**16**) has more respect for its original design (by Marcel Van Coillie) with its wooden joinery.

The names of the architects of numbers 55 and 49 (**17**) unfortunately remain unknown, but they both have a playful quality that is difficult to resist.

17. Plantenstraat 49, unknown (1930s)

Afterwards, turn right onto Frère-Orbanstraat and find number 65 (**18**), by Marcel Colombie, which really stands out, as the door seems so strikingly modern, even though it's originally from the 1930s.

18. Frère-Orbanstraat 65, Marcel Van Coillie (1933)

At the roundabout, head left, and take the first street on your left, the stately Prinsenlaan (**19**). It's easy to see why this is such a princely avenue: the street, which looks out onto the local tennis club, exudes an almost royal quality. Behind it you'll find

Prinsenlaan 21 (1930s)

the Royal Stables, which once belonged to King Leopold II. Hardly surprising then that this street has a great line-up of interesting interbellum houses.

19. Prinsenlaan 60, 21 (1930s)

As you may have noticed, the emphasis up until now has been on art deco, New Objectivity and interbellum architecture in general, as there is a lot of it in this part of Ostend. For the last leg of this tour, however, the focus will shift to 1950s architecture, which is often undervalued, but is just as worthy of your consideration.

Standing in front of the Royal Stables, turn right onto Kaïrostraat and take the third street on your left, Edith Cavellstraat, turn right again onto Filip Van Maestrichtplein, and continue walking down Gentstraat. At number 6 (**20**) you'll find the offices of the former S.E.O. department store by Gaston Eysselinck. The architect who garnered widespread acclaim with his final design, the former Ostend post office (which has since been converted into a cultural centre called De Grote Post), also designed several buildings for a local cooperative, the S.E.O. This organisation was founded in the 1930s by railway employees, to purchase coal. It quickly grew into something bigger and the focus eventually shifted to making available quality goods at affordable prices to the people of Ostend. By the late 1940s, they commissioned a design from Eysselinck for a department store. The first phase – these offices – was built in 1950.

The actual department store opened five years later in 1955 and is located on the other side of these offices, around the corner. To get there, continue walking down Gentstraat, turn right onto Alfons Pieterslaan and then immediately right again onto Romestraat, which you follow until number 11 (**21**). The first department store of its kind in Ostend, it was and still is monumental. In the 1980s, the Mu.ZEE museum was established here. Fortunately, the building was transformed with respect for the original architecture. In fact, it has recently undergone further restoration to enhance Eysselinck's original design (to open it up to the natural light again, by eliminating the walls that were added over the years to display artworks). While the museum is well worth a visit for its architecture, it also houses a wonderful modern art collection.

Tragically, Eysselinck took his own life three years prior to the opening of the department store after multiple setbacks: financial difficulties, marital troubles and his new partner who died from cancer. Aside from these personal tragedies, work-related stress was also a constant source of worry. While building the post office, the tensions between the architect and the client led to Eysselinck ultimately being banned from the site. His death was devastating as the young architect was obviously extremely talented, with a design vernacular that, although heavily inspired by Le Corbusier, was entirely his own. Thankfully, his buildings are now appreciated and valued.

Walk back to Alfons Pieterslaan, cross it, and then continue walking down Leon Spilliaertstraat, where you take the first street on your right, Euphrosina Beernaertstraat. There's no better way to end this tour than with a great example of post-war modernism and interbellum modernism side by side. Number 21B (**22**) is functionalism at its best. Jan Tanghe built this house for his niece in 1957. An incredibly passionate, active (and activist) man, Tanghe lectured at the University of Mons, was an editor of architecture magazine *La Maison*, and the founder of the Groep Planning architects' association, the architecture magazine *A+*, and the nature conservation organisation Bond Beter Leefmilieu. His own home, which you can still find on the outskirts of Ostend, is a testament to his creative and experimental architectural practice.

22. Euphrosina Beernaertstraat 21B, Jan Tanghe (1957)

Number 21A (**23**) is another fine example of New Objectivity by Bernard Christiaens.

To get to the train station, continue walking down Euphrosina Beernaertstraat, turn right onto Christinastraat, then left onto Vindictivelaan, and you'll see the train station on your right.

Liège

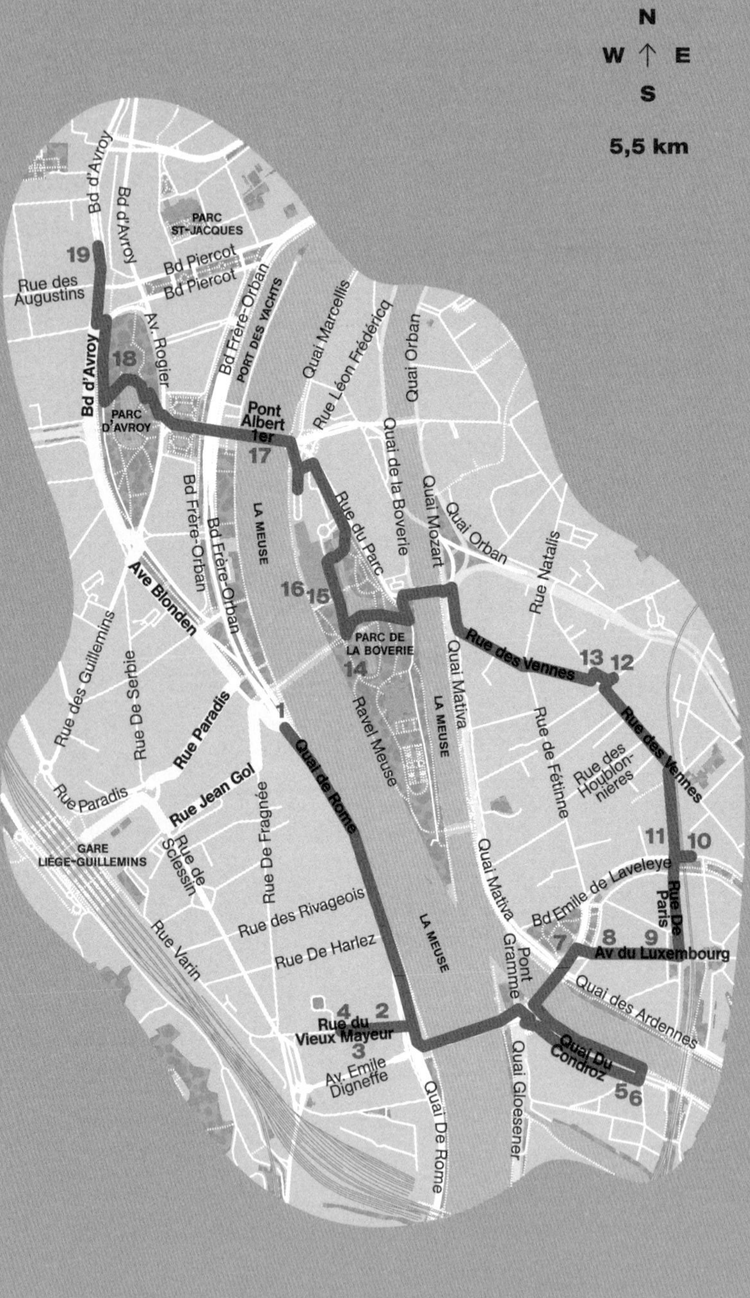
N
W E
S
5,5 km
PARC ST-JACQUES
Bd d'Avroy
Bd Piercot
Rue des Augustins
Av. Rogier
Bd Frère-Orban
PORT DES YACHTS
Quai Marcellis
Rue Léon Frédéricq
Quai Orban
Pont Albert 1er
PARC D'AVROY
LA MEUSE
Rue du Parc
Quai de la Boverie
Quai Mozart
Quai Orban
Rue Natalis
Ave Blonden
PARC DE LA BOVERIE
Rue des Vennes
Rue des Guillemins
Rue De Serbie
Rue Paradis
Ravel Meuse
Quai Mativa
Rue de Fétinne
Rue des Houblonnières
Rue Jean Gol
Quai de Rome
GARE LIÈGE-GUILLEMINS
Rue de Sclessin
Rue De Fragnée
Rue des Rivageois
Rue De Harlez
Rue Varin
Bd Emile de Laveleye
Rue De Paris
Av du Luxembourg
Pont Gramme
Quai des Ardennes
Rue du Vieux Mayeur
Av. Emile Digneffe
Quai Du Condroz
Quai De Rome
Quai Gloesener
1 2 3 4 5 6 7 8 9 10 11 12 13 14 15 16 17 18 19

1 Quai de Rome 1
Louis Rahier
1939

2 Rue du Vieux Mayeur 2
Jean Poskin & Henri Bonhomme
1953-1955

3 Rue du Vieux Mayeur 1
Jean Poskin & Henri Bonhomme
1953-1955

4 Rue du Vieux Mayeur 12-18
Jean Poskin & Henri Bonhomme
1953-1955

5 Quai du Condroz 17
Lucien Speder
1937

6 Quai du Condroz 20
Jean Plumier
1936

7 Avenue Albert Mahiels
Robert Toussaint
1930

8 Avenue Luxembourg 1
Paul Petit
1930

9 Avenue Luxembourg 37
Paul Petit
1939

10 Boulevard Emile de Laveleye 99A
unknown
1930s

11 Rue Saint-Vincent 44
unknown
1936

12 Rue Adrien de Witte 3
Yvon Falise
1932

13 Place Barthélémy Vieillevoye 2
unknown
1930s

14 Volière, Parc de la Boverie
Jean Moutschen
1937

15 Esplanade de l'Europe 2
Groupe L'Equerre
1958

16 Tour Cybernétique, Parc de la Boverie
Nicolas Schöffer
1961

17 Pont Albert 1er
Georges Dedoyard
1957

18 Parc d'Avroy 1
Jean Moutschen
1938

19 Boulevard d'Avroy 96
Jean Moutschen
1938

Liège is often associated with the mining and steel industries, as these brought great prosperity to the region in the 19th and 20th century. This also explains the many stately single-family homes in the city. But there is more to Liège than this. A modern city, Liège has always brought people together, be it through the aforementioned industries or through its university, which was founded in 1817. The city also hosted three (!) world fairs, in 1905, 1930, and 1939 respectively. The plans for the last (and most important) fair were drawn up by local architect Yvon Falise, who received advice from none other than Le Corbusier for this endeavour. The event would go on to have a lasting impact on Liège's urban planning, with some remnants still visible today. After the Second World War, the modernist architecture that popped up in Liège was less oriented towards single family dwellings, consisting for the most part of high-rise blocks of flats and public buildings, as you'll see on this route.

Get off the train at Liège-Guillemins, exit through the main entrance and walk straight ahead, crossing the square with the fountains (Place Pierre Clerdent). You should see Tour Paradis, the shiny skyscraper, loom up in the distance so head in that direction. At 1, Quai de Rome (**1**), you'll find the first stop on this route. This well-kept 1930s block of flats is a good example of fairly straightforward, classical art deco. The wrought iron door and balcony railing have been beautifully preserved, extending the building's past grandeur into the present.

1. Quai de Rome 1, Louis Rahier (1939)

Turn right on Quai de Rome and continue to walk along the Meuse river until you spot the Fragnée bridge ahead. Just before the bridge, on your right, you'll find Rue du Vieux Mayeur and a block of flats by Jean Poskin (**2**), which he designed in collaboration with Henri Bonhomme (it's the blue building on the right). Before you turn the corner, look for the original enamel artwork by Jean Rets on the façade. Art and architecture are often intertwined in modernism, and this is a perfect example.

There's another one just across the road, in Rue du Vieux Mayeur 1 (**3**): a block of flats, also by Poskin, with a beautiful decorative mural at the entrance, signed J. Felix. Poskin was given free rein to design this residence, and as you can see he really flexed his creative skills, with the playful canopy above the entrance as a stand-out feature.

2. Rue du Vieux Mayeur 2, Jean Poskin & Henri Bonhomme (1953-1955), artwork: Jean Rets

3. Rue du Vieux Mayeur 1, Jean Poskin & Henri Bonhomme (1953-1955), artwork: J. Felix

At numbers 12 to 18 (**4**) up the road, you can spot Poskin's signature style again. This is a larger project, with the typical 1950s canopy once again standing out.

4. Rue du Vieux Mayeur 12-18, Jean Poskin & Henri Bonhomme (1953-1955)

Now turn back, walk towards the Fragnée bridge, and cross it. Take the second street on your right, Quai du Condroz, and stop at number 17 (**5**). Chances are you would have stopped to take a closer look anyway as this is a remarkable example of Streamline Moderne, an art deco style of architecture that is characterised by linear elements and curved forms.

5. Quai du Condroz 17, Lucien Speder (1937)

Numbers 18 and 19 were designed in the same vein but underwent more alterations. Fortunately, number 20 (**6**) has been preserved in its original state. The assumption is that the architect Jean Plumier designed this house for himself, as it has room for a spacious office and waiting room on the ground floor. The curves in the façade are extended in the interior, with rooms and built-in furniture designed to fit its circular shape. At the time of writing, the house had just recently changed hands, so we can only guess what will become of this curvy cutie. 6. Quai du Condroz 20, Jean Plumier (1936)

Turn around and walk back to the bridge, then turn right and cross the river. You should see St Vincent's Church (**7**), which was designed by Robert Toussaint and built for the 1930 World Fair, to your left. The best way to get a clear view of this building is to admire it from afar. The interior can only be seen during Mass. The young Toussaint won the competition for its creation just five years after graduating from the Academy of Fine Arts of Liège. The church was built from reinforced concrete, which was a new material at the time. Toussaint was clearly influenced by the Basilica of Koekelberg (Albert Van huffel, 1927) for the design of his most significant work.

Cross the street and walk on the right-hand side of Avenue Albert Mahiels, to the right of the trees. On the corner with Avenue du Luxembourg, you will run into an art deco block of flats from 1923 with Renaissance influences (**8**). This was one of the first high-rises to be built in Wallonia. The architect of this project was Paul Petit, and the building was intended for bourgeois families, with rooms in the attics for their servants. Walk down Avenue du Luxembourg to see the building up close.

At number 37 (**9**) you will find another block of flats by Petit, from 1937. The design is much more austere, and devoid of any ornamentation, with a very minimal façade. The glass bricks above the back door (around the corner) and the minimalist albeit figurative grilles on the doors stand out in particular. The block of flats had modern amenities that were considered quite novel in those days, such as fully-equipped Cubex kitchens (which are a design classic today), telephones for calling one's servants, lifts, etc. High-rises and living high above the city were all the rage at the time. By the 1930s, the fascination with this style of living only served to confer status on the highest floors, which were reserved for the happy few.

Take the second street on your left, Rue de Paris, and then the first on your right, Boulevard Emile de Laveleye, and walk to number 99A (**10**). While the building has seen better times, it's worth seeing through its general shabbiness to distinguish the lovely details. The terrace with its curved windows, the decorative ironwork, and the beautiful, tiled columns are all hidden gems.

10. Boulevard Emile de Laveleye 99A, unknown (1930s)

Walk back to the corner with Rue de Paris, turn right onto Rue Saint Vincent, and then stop at number 44 (**11**). We have no information about the architect, which only adds to the mystery that surrounds this original treasure. Check out the striking wooden joinery!

11. Rue Saint-Vincent 44, unknown (1936)

Continue walking down Rue Saint Vincent and turn left onto Rue des Vennes. Now take the next street on your right, Place Barthélémy Vieillevoye, then go right again on Rue Adrien de Witte, where you should stop at number 3 (**12**). Unfortunately, the original door of this house by Yvon Falise has since been replaced. Despite this alteration, this is a perfect example of pure, functionalist modernism at its best. Thanks to his design for the 1939 World Fair, Falise played an indispensable part in Liège's architectural history. But well before this, he'd already made his mark when he initiated a magazine called *L'Équerre* in 1928 while still at the Academy. *L'Équerre* was the successor to the *7 Arts* magazine (see chapter on Uccle) and was founded by Falise, Jean Moutschen, Émile Parent, and several other students at Liège's Academy of Fine Arts. The group had radical ideas and criticised the academicism that prevailed in Liège's urbanism, architecture and art. What started out as a student publication soon became a powerful propaganda tool for the modernist movement in Liège and Belgium. Their appointment as the secretariat of the Belgian section of the CIAM (Congrès Internationaux d'Architecture Moderne – International Congresses of Modern Architecture) in 1935 is an indication of just how progressive the group had become. The house at number 3 was built just two years after Falise graduated from the academy and is essentially a summary of all the principles of *L'Équerre*: functionalism, economy, standardisation, and the rejection of ornamentation.

Turn back and take a right on Place Barthélémy Vieillevoye. Number 2 (**13**), with its alternate use of bricks, glass bricks, and tiles, and its beautiful grilles on the door and window, is a good example of art deco of the interbellum.

Cross the square and turn right on Rue des Vennes. Walk to the end of the street, then turn right on Quai Julien-Remont. Take a left, crossing the bridge, and walk to the park. Keep left until you spot the large bridge across the park ahead. Take the path to the right of the bridge and cross the pond to get to the old aviary (**14**), which was designed by Jean

Moutschen, another member of *L'Équerre*. This is one of the remaining buildings of the former zoo that used to be in the park. 14. Volière, Parc de la Boverie, Jean Moutschen (1937)

You can see more of *L'Équerre's* output just around the corner. Look to your right to spot the Palais des Congrès de Liège (**15**), a conference centre that was designed in the 1950s by Groupe L'Équerre. As its name suggests, the group had become an actual architecture firm by then. Moutschen and Falise had already left, but the rest of *L'Équerre*'s founding members were still on board. The construction of this building was part of a general renewal of Liège's infrastructure in light of the upcoming Expo 58 (the World Fair in Brussels). The Palais des Congrès, which is situated on the banks of the Meuse river, is a recognisable landmark of Liège, with panoramic windows that look out onto the water. Like their contemporaries, the Groupe L'Équerre believed in the marriage between architecture and art, which is why you'll find several artworks both in- and outside of the building. Walk around it to spot the mosaic by Eva Herbiet at the side entrance and a sculpture by Freddy Wybaux on the north façade, near the main entrance.

15. Palais des Congrès, Esplanade de l'Europe 2, Groupe L'Equerre (1958)

But before you do this, have a look at the 52-metre-tall Tour Cybernétique (Cyber Tower) (**16**) to your left, which was built here three years after the completion of the conference centre, and is another city landmark. This abstract work was designed by the French-Hungarian Nicolas Schöffer, perhaps the first ever attempt at "cybernetic" art. The tower is in constant movement and is controlled by various parameters of the urban environment (light, rain, wind, temperature, noise level, humidity, etc.). Probes throughout the city send messages to the tower's "brain", which is then activated. Only in Liège!

Once you have arrived on the other side of the Palais des Congrès, exit the park onto the aptly named Rue du Parc, and turn left. Before you know it, you'll find yourself on the Albert Ier bridge (**17**). After being sabotaged during the Second World War to slow the advance of German troops, a permanent structure by Georges Dedoyard was built here in 1957. Once again, notice the juxtaposition of art and architecture, and the sculptures by Pierre Caille and George Grard.

17. Pont Albert 1er, Georges Dedoyard (1957), sculpture: George Grard

Once you have crossed the bridge, keep walking until you reach Parc d'Avroy (Avroy Park). Enter the park and turn right, then follow the signs for the Trinkhall Museum. Look for the bandstand opposite the museum (**18**). Another design by Jean Moutschen for the 1939 World Fair, this bandstand has been preserved intact and is still in use today.

18. Parc d'Avroy 1, Jean Moutschen (1938)

With your back to the museum, turn right and continue to the end of the footpath. Cross the street at the zebra crossing, then go left again at another zebra crossing, walking towards the Église du Saint-Sacrement (Church of the Holy Sacrament). Turn right onto Boulevard d'Avroy. Continue walking until you reach number 96, the Athénée Léonie de Waha (**19**), and the last stop on this route. This monumental school from 1938 is Jean Moutschen's undisputed masterpiece. The building catered to contemporary needs with spaces that were deemed exceptional at the time: an 850-seat auditorium, a 2,400-m^2 playground, a boarding school, laboratories, a music room, gymnasiums,

Athénée Léonie de Waha, Boulevard d'Avroy 96, Jean Moutschen (1938)

Athénée Léonie de Waha, Boulevard d'Avroy 96, Jean Moutschen (1938)

a swimming pool, and even an underground shelter for a thousand people. Everything was designed with the comfort of the pupils and teachers in mind. Moutschen commissioned frescoes, mosaics, paintings, and stained-glass windows from local artists (twenty artworks in total). His idea was to give pupils an opportunity to be in daily contact with an environment with a more artistic dimension. As you can see, Moutschen clearly succeeded in his mission.

19. Athénée Léonie de Waha, Boulevard d'Avroy 96, Jean Moutschen (1938)

To return to the train station, walk back down Boulevard d'Avroy, past the park, until it becomes Avenue Blonden. Take the second street on your right, Rue Paradis, which will lead you right back to where you started.

Turnhout

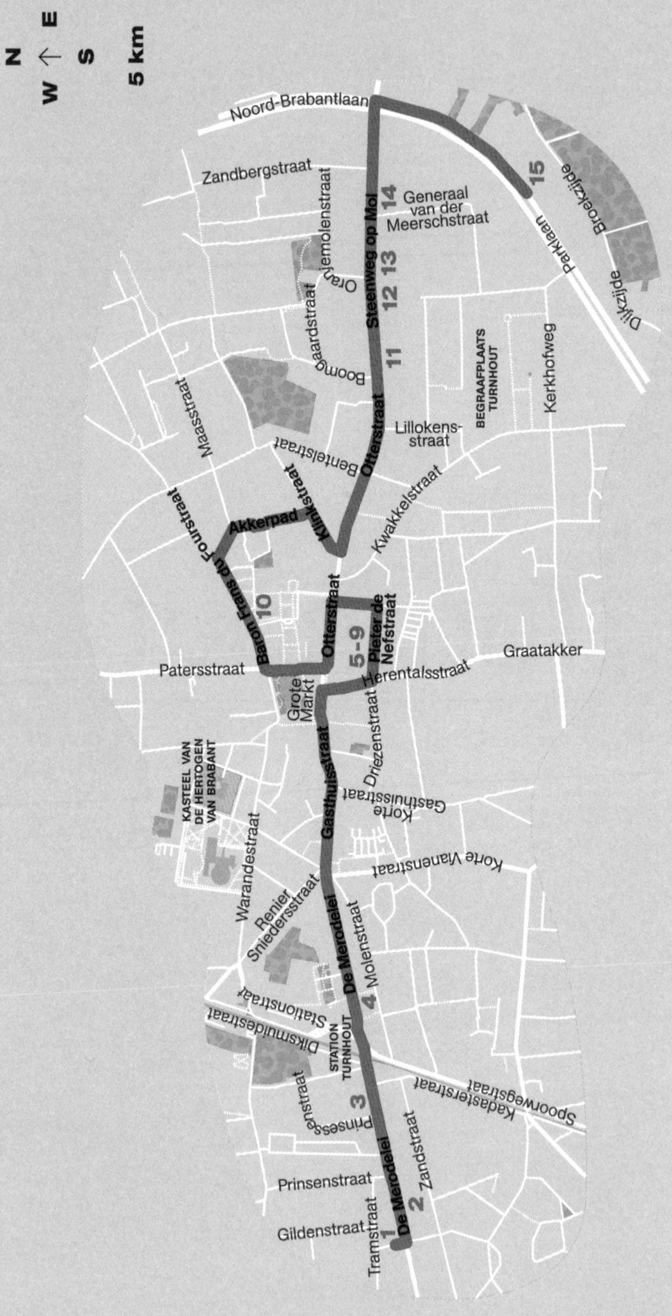
N
W
E
S
5 km
Noord-Brabantlaan
Zandbergstraat
Oranjemolenstraat
Steenweg op Mol
14
Generaal van der Meerschstraat
13
12
11
15
Parklaan
Broekzijde
Dijkzijde
Boomgaardstraat
BEGRAAFPLAATS TURNHOUT
Kerkhofweg
Lillokensstraat
Otterstraat
Maasstraat
Bentelstraat
Klinkstraat
Akkerpad
Kwakkelstraat
Baron Frans du Fourstraat
10
Otterstraat
Pieter de Nefstraat
5-9
Graatakker
Patersstraat
Herentalsstraat
Grote Markt
Driezenstraat
KASTEEL VAN DE HERTOGEN VAN BRABANT
Gasthuisstraat
Korte Gasthuisstraat
Korte Vianenstraat
Warandestraat
Renier Sniedersstraat
De Merodelei
Molenstraat
4
Stationstraat
Diksmuidestraat
STATION TURNHOUT
Spoorwegstraat
Kadasterstraat
3
Prinsesstraat
Prinsenstraat
Zandstraat
De Merodelei
2
Gildenstraat
1
Tramstraat

1 Onze Lieve Vrouwstraat 2
Jean Hendrickx
1939

2 De Merodelei 187
Ernest Wauters
1932

3 De Merodelei 114
Charles Gauquie
1939

4 De Merodelei 65
Carli Vanhout & Paul Schellekens
1964

5 Pieter De Nefstraat 9
unknown
1930s

6 Pieter De Nefstraat 11
Eduard Van Steenbergen
1941

7 Pieter De Nefstraat 17
Eduard Van Steenbergen
1941

8 Pieter De Nefstraat 27
unknown
1930s

9 Pieter De Nefstraat 33
unknown
1939

10 Baron Frans du Fourstraat 17
Jacques Saintenoy
1937

11 Steenweg op Mol 16
unknown
1930s

12 Steenweg op Mol 48
Ernest Wauters
1932

13 Steenweg op Mol 54
Jos Eelens
1934

14 Steenweg op Mol 66
Jozef Schellekens
1934

15 Parklaan 146
Carli Vanhout & Paul Schellekens
1964

In the heart of the Kempen region, you will find Turnhout, a smallish city that has lots to offer, architecturally speaking. Perhaps the Turnhout School rings a bell? With their fresh designs, this group of young architects changed the face of mid-century design in Turnhout. Or perhaps you've heard of Jozef Schellekens and his perfectly preserved 1930s home, that's part of the Iconic Houses network? If not, then you probably wouldn't immediately associate this provincial city with innovative architecture. But now you are here, and there's lots to discover, so start walking!

One thing to bear in mind before you set off: this walking tour is not a loop, meaning you will have to walk all the way back. But you know what they say about getting your 10,000 steps a day!

Get off the bus at Turnhout Stelplaats, walk down De Merodelei leaving the train station behind you, and take the third street on your right, Onze Lieve Vrouwstraat. At number 2 (**1**) you will find an art deco beauty designed by the Brussels architect Jean Hendrickx. Although some of the joinery has unfortunately been renewed, the grille on the door, which features a playful pattern, has been preserved. With the house to your left, return to De Merodelei, then cross the street and turn left, until you reach number 187 (**2**). You'll notice that the house next to it features an exact copy of the façade; these houses once belonged to the Verreet brothers, who originally hailed from Germany and who were prominent figures in the port industry. When they asked local architect Ernest Wauters to design their homes, no expense was spared. Number 187 is in largely original condition and features walnut and rosewood wall panelling, a striking staircase with a built-in bench and stained-glass windows throughout. At the back lie the (more modest, but surprisingly spacious) servants' quarters. If you have time, do have a look at Zandstraat 76 around the corner, where you can see the façade of these quarters, in a style that is reminiscent of the Amsterdam School.

2. De Merodelei 187, Ernest Wauters (1932)

De Merodelei 187, Ernest Wauters (1932)

Continue walking down De Merodelei until you reach number 114 on your left (**3**), an elegant example of art deco. The juxtaposition of the yellow brick with the door's soft yellow tones, and the flower relief around it lend the building a poetic quality, making it stand out from other houses of the same period on this street.

3. De Merodelei 114, Charles Gauquie (1939)

While you make your way to your next stop at De Merodelei 65, let's take a quick, closer look at the Turnhout School, whose members designed this building.

In the 1960s, Turnhout was home to several young architects, who would go on to change the face of this city forever. They included Lou Jansen & Rudi Schiltz, Paul Neefs, and Carli Vanhout & Paul Schellekens. Their work was both innovative and modern and they mainly looked to Scandinavian architecture, as well as their travels through the U.S., for inspiration. They studied the work of Frank Lloyd Wright, Eero Saarinen, Alvar Aalto, Mies van der Rohe, Le Corbusier and many others. Although they all worked around the same time and shared a common ground, they did not become their influences (nor did they look to each other for inspiration), retaining their architectural individuality throughout their careers. They did not have a group identity per se, but it was Renaat Braem who first considered them as a group in a magazine article in 1976. The term "Turnhout School" was only coined in 1995, when these architects and their unique contribution to the Belgian architectural landscape were finally recognised and acknowledged. As their buildings all happen to be located closer to the centre of Turnhout, this tour will only take you past work by Vanhout and Schellekens.

After graduation, Carli Vanhout started his own practice. Paul Schellekens, his brother-in-law, joined him a few years later. Initially, Schellekens assisted Vanhout as a draughtsman, as he was still at school. In between studying and working for Vanhout, Schellekens took many trips to study and discover architecture, his journeys taking him all over Europe and as far as India, Mexico and the U.S. Fuelled by these international experiences, he returned full of progressive ideas, and eventually became a partner in the firm.

On to number 65 (**4**) then. This former office from 1964 is one of their earliest collaborations but because of the use of visible (albeit painted) concrete, it already has that brutalist feel that would characterise so much of their later work. Although no longer used as an office, the building's outlook has remained unchanged.

4. De Merodelei 65, Carli Vanhout & Paul Schellekens (1964)

Continue walking until De Merodelei turns into Gasthuisstraat and later Grote Markt, then take the first street on your right, Herentalsstraat, and the first on your left, Pieter De Nefstraat. You'll notice that this street is lined with several interbellum buildings; it was built in 1936, on the grounds of the former St. Joseph school.

Your first stop on this street: number 9 (**5**). As the architect is unknown, there's not much to add, but do look at the narrow tiles on the façade and the beautiful ironwork on the door.

Number 11 (**6**), on the other hand, is signed by the architect himself, none other than Eduard Van Steenbergen, one of Antwerp's most celebrated modernist architects of the interbellum period. For some reason, Van Steenbergen designed several houses for doctors (with space for their practice) in Turnhout between 1939 and 1941. While number 11 perhaps isn't Van Steenbergen's most exciting or progressive work, the combination of different materials on the façade (plastering, brick, and natural stone) makes it interesting. Number 17 (**7**), also by Van Steenbergen, was built for a doctor as well. The sheer width of both premises stands out, as they had to house waiting rooms and consulting rooms as well as space to live. Van Steenbergen was also an interior designer and inside you can see mantelpieces, staircases, stained-glass windows, which he also designed. Each interior is slightly different, reflecting his clients' taste.

Next up is another anonymous design, at number 27 (**8**). Once a great example of the New Objectivity, it has sadly fallen into disrepair in recent years, with its façade now overgrown with ivy. Thankfully, someone has recently taken on this sizeable project and here's hoping that the house's beauty will soon be revealed to us again in all its glory.

8. Pieter De Nefstraat 27, unknown (1930s)

Three doors down, you will find another anonymous example of interbellum modernism (**9**). The architect's name was originally inscribed in a tile on the façade, but it fell off during a storm and was irreparable. As a result, his identity remains shrouded in mystery. The typically Belgian yellow brick steals the show here, along with the elegant wrought iron door and stained-glass windows. Inside, many period details have been preserved, with the all-marbrite pink bathroom as the showstopper.

Turn left onto Beekstraat, left again onto Otterstraat and then right onto Grote Markt. The next street on your right, Baron Frans du Fourstraat, leads you to your next stop, the former Brepols offices at number 17 (**10**), which are now home to the city's art academy. In the 19th century, Turnhout became the centre of the Belgian paper industry, and Brepols was its biggest player. The historical Brepols mill and offices were situated around Grote Markt and this street, and the building you see here dates from 1937. It features a façade in austere red brick

Pieter De Nefstraat 33, unknown (1930s)

and concrete and was designed by the renowned Brussels architect Jacques Saintenoy, who built several modernist flats. The New Objectivity-style interior is characterised by monumentality, transparency, and light, culminating in the large room on the first floor, which features double-height windows, a wraparound gallery with tubular railings, granite floors, and glazed fine-steel partitions. Its restoration (and the building of a new section on the other side) was completed in 2021 and it's a perfect example of a successful repurposing, that will hopefully set the tone for the restoration of similar modernist buildings that are in a state of disrepair.

10. Baron Frans du Fourstraat 17, Jacques Saintenoy (1937)

Now it's time for a bit of a walk to get to the last leg of this tour. Continue walking down Baron Frans du Fourstraat, turn right onto Schoolstraat, and then right again onto Akkerpad. At the top of this street, turn right onto Klinkstraat, and then left onto Otterstraat, which turns into Steenweg op Mol. Number 16 (**11**) may not be that innovative in terms of design, but the playful wrought ironwork on the windows and front door is remarkable.

Walk past the garages and stop at number 48 (**12**), by Ernest Wauters, from the early 1930s. The bright colours and combination of different materials immediately strike the eye and it's worth stopping for a moment to take in all the details. If not for the current owners, this mansion might have been razed to the ground, as it had not been listed as heritage. As you may recall from our second stop, the architect Ernest Wauters was a creative architect who also designed interiors. This house is a perfect example of the cubist-expressionist style that would go on to become his trademark, with colourfully tiled fireplaces, stained-glass windows, and Wauters' distinctive sawtooth pattern (as you can see on the façade).

12. Steenweg op Mol 48, Ernest Wauters (1932)

From cubism to functionalism at our next stop, number 54 (**13**). This design by Jos Eelens is stripped of any superfluous details, exuding an austere quality that is strong in its simplicity. This house also has links to Turnhout's printing industry, as the client was the writer and publisher Jozef Simons, who worked for the printer's to the left of the house. Initially, Eelens conceived the house as a double dwelling for Simons and the owner of the printing company, but only this house was built. Thankfully, it has stayed in the family and has been perfectly preserved.

13. Steenweg op Mol 54, Jos Eelens (1934)

At number 66 (**14**) you can see another double dwelling, the house of Jozef Schellekens, from 1934. Although it is not the last stop of this route, it is definitely the cherry on the cake. Jozef Schellekens was born and bred in Turnhout and passionate about the Kempen region and its architecture. He started out his career working as a draughtsman for local architect Jules Taeymans, who encouraged him to combine his job with his architectural studies.

The dwelling you see here was built for himself and for his friend, the actor Theo Op de Beeck, who was to live at number 64 (the building to the right of it). Schellekens was only 24 when it was built and had just started his own architectural practice, which was located on the ground floor, next to the entrance. It was one of the first modernist buildings in the area and the exterior features the typical glazing and metal joinery that is characteristic of the New Objectivity style. The interior has vibrant (yet harmonious) colours, tiles, marbrite, and natural stone, and includes a mural by Schellekens (he was also a talented painter) in the kitchen. The young family soon moved in, but tragedy struck when the couple's fourth child was born and his wife passed away. Schellekens suddenly found himself a young widower and a single father. He remarried soon after, but his new life partner did not care for the ultra-modern house and succeeded in covering up the entire interior, even going as far as adding a level in the entry hall so the space lost its monumentality. Years passed and in 2012, it was restored to its former glory. Today it looks every bit as modern as it did almost 100 years ago.

14. Steenweg op Mol 66, Jozef Schellekens (1934)

Steenweg op Mol 66, Jozef Schellekens (1934)

Steenweg op Mol 66, Jozef Schellekens (1934)

Steenweg op Mol 66, Jozef Schellekens (1934)

As you may have guessed by the name, Paul Schellekens, of Vanhout & Schellekens, was Jozef's son. Your walk ends at the former offices of Vanhout & Schellekens. Follow Steenweg op Mol to the intersection, cross the street, and turn right onto Parklaan. Walk to number 146 (**15**). Would you look at that façade! Due to its horizontality, the building is beautifully integrated into its surroundings. Today, the front of the building is still home to an architectal practice (co-owned by Luc, Carli Vanhout's son), while the rear originally served as Carli Vanhout's family home. The two are separated by a patio in the middle.

15. Parklaan 146, Carli Vanhout & Paul Schellekens (1964)

Parklaan 146, Carli Vanhout & Paul Schellekens (1964)

Tournai

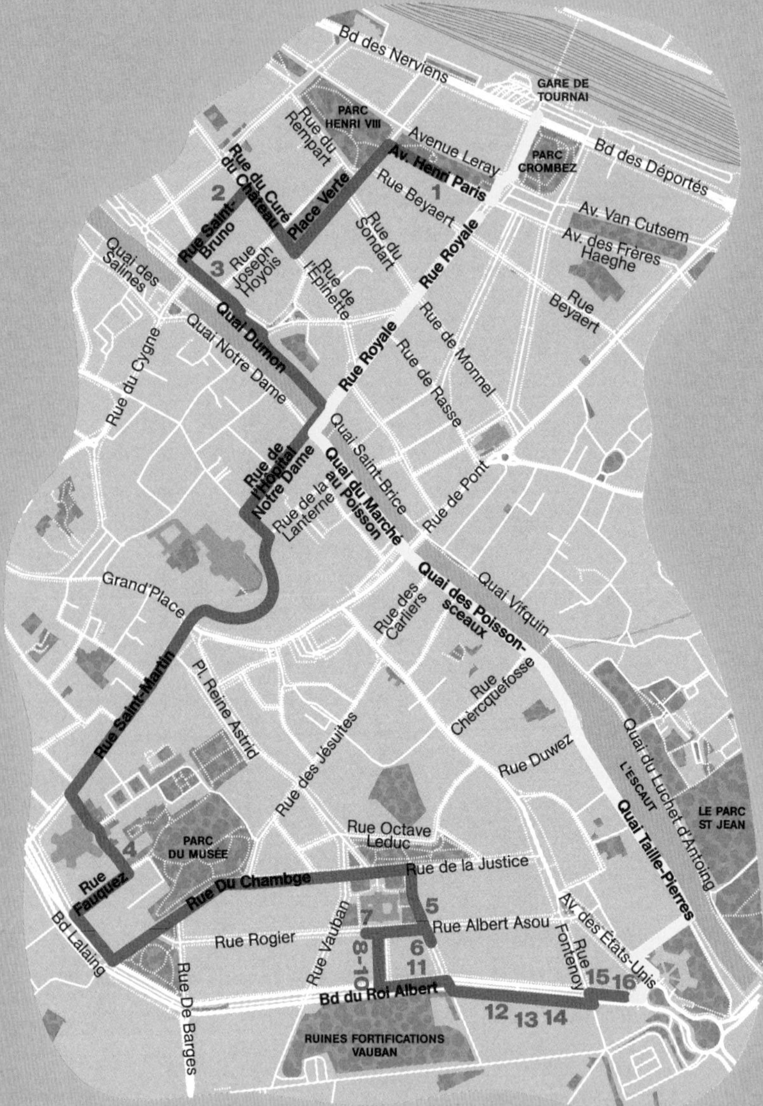
Bd des Nerviens
GARE DE TOURNAI
PARC HENRI VIII
Rue du Rempart
Avenue Leray
Av. Henri Paris
PARC CROMBEZ
Bd des Déportés
Rue du Curé du Château
Place Verte
Rue Beyaert
Av. Van Cutsem
Av. des Frères Haeghe
Rue Saint-Bruno
Rue Joseph Hoyois
Rue du Sondart
Rue Royale
Quai des Salines
Rue de l'Epinette
Rue Beyaert
Quai Dumon
Quai Notre Dame
Rue de Monnel
Rue du Cygne
Rue de Rasse
Rue de l'Hôpital Notre Dame
Quai Saint-Brice
Rue de Pont
Rue de la Lanterne
Quai du Marché au Poisson
Grand'Place
Quai Vifquin
Rue des Carliers
Quai des Poissonceaux
Rue Chèrcquefosse
Pl. Reine Astrid
Rue Saint-Martin
Rue des Jésuites
Rue Duwez
Quai du Luchet d'Antoing
L'ESCAUT
Quai Taille-Pierres
LE PARC ST JEAN
Rue Octave Leduc
PARC DU MUSÉE
Rue de la Justice
Rue Fauquez
Rue Du Chambge
Rue Albert Asou
Rue Rogier
Rue Vauban
Av. des États-Unis
Rue Fontenoy
Bd Lalaing
Rue De Barges
Bd du Roi Albert
RUINES FORTIFICATIONS VAUBAN
1
2
3
4
5
6
7
8-10
11
12
13
14
15
16

N
W ↑ E
S

3,5 km

1 Avenue Henri Paris 13
Louis Gaudemont
1938

2 Rue Saint-Bruno 13
François Ladavid
1936

3 Quai Dumon 10
Robert Schotte
1962

4 Rue de l'Enclos
Saint-Martin 18
Henri Lacoste
1935

5 Rue du Général Ruquoy 10
Charles Schelstraete
1937

6 Rue du Général Ruquoy 1
unknown
1930s

7 Rue Albert Asou 74
unknown
1930s

8 Av. du 3ème Chasseurs
à Pied 1
Géo Bariseau
1930s

9 Av. du 3ème Chasseurs
à Pied 9
Emile Delepierre
1935

10 Av. du 3ème Chasseurs
à Pied 11
Jos & Dés. De Smet
1935

11 Boulevard du Roi Albert 82
unknown
1933

12 Boulevard du Roi Albert 45
unknown
1930s

13 Boulevard du Roi Albert 33
François Ladavid
1936

14 Boulevard du Roi Albert 25
Géo Bariseau
1934

15 Boulevard du Roi Albert 20
Géo Bariseau
1930s

16 Boulevard du Roi Albert 16
Géo Bariseau
1930s

Tournai lies on the Belgian-French border, so you could be forgiven for thinking that you're in France instead of Belgium when you visit it. Historically, Tournai also has links with Picardy, and the Picard language, which is still spoken by some in northern France and part of Wallonia in Belgium, is lasting evidence of this former union. Tournai is home to several UNESCO World Heritage Sites. Most of these Gothic or Romanesque sites date from the Middle Ages but the city is also well known for its art nouveau buildings.

What few people know, however, is that Tournai also has several impressive art deco buildings, which this route will focus on.

With your back to the train station's main entrance, head towards Place Crombez, leaving the park on your left. Take the second street on your right, Avenue Henri Paris, and walk to number 13 (**1**). This marvellously preserved house by Louis Gaudemont is a textbook example of modernism, with the architect clearly looking to Le Corbusier for inspiration. Note the balcony, the horizontality of the windows, and the roof terrace that connects the outside with the inside. You can tell by the round windows, orange tiles, and the elegant grille on the door that Gaudemont also embraced the art deco aesthetic.

Continue your walk down Avenue Henri Paris until you reach the park, then turn left onto Place Verte. Take the second on your right, Rue de l'Epinette, which soon turns into Rue du Curé du Château. Then take the second street on your left, Rue Saint-Bruno, and stop at number 13 (**2**). This house, which dates from around the same period as your previous stop and has a similar colour scheme, is full-on art deco. Local architect François Ladavid designed this home for himself and visibly decided to pull out all the stops. The façade incorporates just about every decorative element imaginable, and it works like a charm. Note how many different types of glass he used. The cimorné above the door and below the roof adds a graphic element, and then there are the chunky tiles and slim window frames, which, despite being different shades of green, are in perfect harmony. Those same shades of green return in the interior, for the door frames, floor tiles, stairs, and even the heating elements. These are just a few of the original features that have been retained, along with the fireplaces, an integrated sculpture by local artist Nelly Mercier, an impressive stairwell, and much more. Based on this house, you may think that Ladavid was a renowned architect in Tournai. Unfortunately, very little information can be found about him, and it's painful to imagine what this could mean for the preservation of his stunning work. It's about time he gets the recognition he deserves.

2. Rue Saint-Bruno 13, François Ladavid (1936)

At the top of Rue Saint-Bruno, turn left onto Quai Dumon and stop at number 10, the former home of architect Robert Schotte, and the only post-war building on this route (**3**). As you may have guessed from his name, Schotte, who originally hailed from Ghent, was Flemish. After his architecture studies at Saint Luc (where he was later employed as a teacher) in Tournai, he decided to stay here. As you walk along Quai Dumon, your attention is immediately drawn to this clean, white, functionalist façade that stands out among the 19th-century townhouses that line the street. Schotte lived (on the upper floors) and worked (on the ground floor) here. In true modernist fashion, the rear opens up completely onto the garden. While the ground-floor spaces don't get a lot of light, the house literally bathes in it from the first floor up. After Schotte's death, the house stayed in the family. It remains completely intact and is well kept. The kitchen is located on the first floor, behind the square window to your right. To the left of the kitchen, the architect added an open-plan living room, separated by a spiral staircase from the veranda that takes up the entire width of the back of the house. The bedrooms are on the second floor. With period furniture by Knoll, among others, you can get a clear idea of what life would have been like in the 1960s. Here's hoping the house is preserved for future generations.

3. Quai Dumon 10, Robert Schotte (1962)

Quai Dumon 10, Robert Schotte (1962)

Quai Dumon 10, Robert Schotte (1962)

Follow Quai Dumon along the river until it turns into Quai Saint-Brice, then walk across Notre Dame bridge and continue straight on until Tournai's famed Cathedral looms up before you. Keep left as you walk around the cathedral towards the belfry, the tall tower behind it. With the belfry on your right, cross the street and continue down Rue Saint-Martin. Take the third street on your left, called Rue de l'Enclos Saint-Martin. Walk through the gate that has "Musee des Beaux Arts" painted on it and past the Museum of Fine Arts (by Victor Horta, also worth visiting) until you reach number 18 (**4**). This is definitely the most enigmatic building on this route. While not completely modernist, it is worth including it nonetheless, because of its architect, Henry Lacoste, a figurehead of Belgian architecture during the interbellum. By 1935, the curator of the Fine Arts Museum had become the owner of this former abbey and he decided to have Lacoste renovate and expand it. Lacoste, a local, had travelled far and wide. After his studies in Brussels and Paris in the early 1900s, he participated in archaeological excavations in Delphi and Baghdad, among other places. This provided him with extensive inspiration, and his fascination for ancient civilisations is apparent in his designs. His work, however, also definitely has an art deco slant to it, which explains its kinship with modernism. The building appears to be closed off from the street but walk a little further and take a peek behind the wall, and you'll realise that it actually opens up onto the garden, a typically modernist approach. Lacoste also designed several interior elements, but it is unclear whether these have been preserved.

4. Rue de l'Enclos Saint-Martin 18, Henri Lacoste (1935)

Turn right onto Rue Fauquez, then left on Boulevard Lalaing, and left again on Rue du Chambge, which you follow until it turns into Place du Palais de Justice, and then Rue de la Justice. On Rue de la Justice, take the first street on your right, Rue du Général Ruquoy, and stop at number 10 (**5**). You're in luck, because the house's façade was recently completely restored. You can tell that its architect Charles Schelstraete had a soft spot for art deco, and that he also added unique elements to its design vocabulary. Schelstraete paid equal attention to the interior, creating a marble entrance, decorative wooden floors, curved doors, and graphic stained glass.

5. Rue du Général Ruquoy 10, Charles Schelstraete (1937)

With your back to number 10, turn left and walk to number 1 on the corner for more recently renovated modernism (**6**).

Instead of following Rue du Général Ruquoy, head back and turn left onto Rue Albert Asou, then walk to number 74 (**7**). Perhaps not as well kept but almost completely original, the style of this anonymous house is more akin to Streamline Moderne, especially if you look at the right top corner of its façade.

7. Rue Albert Asou 74, unknown (1930s)

To the left of it, on the corner with Avenue du 3ème Chasseurs à Pied, lies the first of several Géo Bariseau designs that you'll run into (**8**). And what a stunner it is! Géo Bariseau is Georges Bariseau junior, and not his father, whose name was also Georges, and who also was an architect to complicate matters even more. In any event, the way in which Bariseau combined different volumes, materials, and forms, and still managed to create a balanced design, is nothing short of a feat. Even his signature at the bottom right of the entrance is a tiny work of art. Together with Ladavid, Bariseau was one of the main architects of renewal in Tournai in the years between the two World Wars. Many of their works can be found in this neighbourhood, one of a few in the city where they only started building in the 1930s, leaving us with a nice example of period architecture. To understand this late development, it's worth taking a closer look at Tournai's urban planning history: the area was cleared in 1877, after the city decided to demolish its city walls. Gas and electricity were only laid in 1932.

8. Av. du 3ème Chasseurs à Pied 1, Géo Bariseau (1930s)

Other noteworthy modernist houses on this street are numbers 9 (**9**) and 11 (**10**), which both have beautiful, original ironwork on the doors.

9. Av. du 3ème Chasseurs à Pied 9, Emile Delepierre (1935)

On to Boulevard du Roi Albert for the final leg of the route, a street that is lined with lots of interesting examples of Tournai modernism. At the time this spacious, leafy boulevard was built for the upper classes who had the means to build homes here. Cars were definitely not as ubiquitous as they are today. To get a better idea of what this area would have looked like at the time, try to imagine it without cars.

Turn left and walk to number 82 (**11**) for your first, anonymous, stop on Boulevard du Roi Albert. While the house was partly renovated, it still features some original details, especially around the door and entrance. Although the architect is unknown, the year of construction has been inscribed in the façade. Try and find it!

11. Boulevard du Roi Albert 82, unknown (1933)

Now cross the street to explore the other side of the boulevard. First up: number 45 (**12**), by another unknown architect. It is somewhat concealed by the plantings, so you'll have to make an effort to get a closer look. It's remarkable for its original, graphic details, such as the ironwork on the door and fence, the woodwork on the garage door and, last but not least, the impressive ornamental top part of the façade.

12. Boulevard du Roi Albert 45, unknown (1930s)

Next up: number 33 (**13**), signed François Ladavid. Even here, on this remarkable street, Ladavid's design stands out and feels fresh, something that is entirely due to the materials used. By adding tiles to the façade, he has succeeded in creating depth and giving it an illustrative character, which makes for an original take on modernism.

13. Boulevard du Roi Albert 33, François Ladavid (1936)

The last three stops were all designed by Géo Bariseau. Start at number 25 (**14**), which is a riot of colour. Though it's doubtful that the joinery was originally painted this shade of yellow, at least it's been preserved. Perhaps the tiles at the entrance are a better indication of the original colour scheme. Either way, it's a joyous, expressive design, full of details that all seem to contribute to a composition that is similar to an abstract painting. Just notice how the abstract shapes pop up in the stained glass above the door – genius! Bariseau used many of these recurring elements in his designs. Fortunately, there are several nearby so you can compare.

14. Boulevard du Roi Albert 25, Géo Bariseau (1934)

Cross the boulevard again to arrive at number 20 (**15**), with references to both the Amsterdam School (the brickwork) and the Streamline Moderne style (the curves and porthole windows). The upper part of the façade is conceived as two symmetrical halves, while the lower part is more expressive. Bariseau seems to have settled on a round motif, with curved edges (did you notice the gorgeous built-in planters to the left of the door?), curved railing, round windows, and spherical stone decoration in front of the stained glass.

15. Boulevard du Roi Albert 20, Géo Bariseau (1930s)

And just like that, you've arrived at your last stop, just two doors down, at number 16 (**16**). It's a shame that they've replaced the garage door as this house is a perfect marriage between the last two Bariseau designs in every respect.

It's obvious that Bariseau was at the top of his game during the years in between the two World Wars, and we're lucky that we can still admire his work almost 100 years later. Let's hope that people can enjoy his designs for another 100 years at least!

Take the next street on your left, Avenue des États Unis, to walk back to the train station. Then immediately turn right onto Rue Tour Canteraine. Take a left at the river, which you follow until the third bridge on your right. Cross the bridge and keep going straight. You'll see the train station in the distance.

Deurne (Antwerp)

DRAKENHOF
Mortselsesteenweg
Eksterlaar
Eksterlaar
Oudedonklaan
17
16
Unitaslaan
Unitaslaan
Sint-
Rochusstraat
Dascottelei
Vroenhofstraat
Menegemlei
BOEKENBERGPARK
Eduard van
Steenbergenlaan
15
Drakenhoflaan
Waalhofstraat
Bauscheitlaan
24
14
18
19
Van
21
-
23
20
Boekenberglei
Drakenhoflaan
Boekenberglei
13
Muggenberglei
6
7
Ravelsbergstraat
Basseliersstraat
8
9
Van Notenstraat
Knyffstraat
De Borrekensstraat
Jozef Verbovenlei
Joos Robijnslei
10
Cruyslei
11
Gitschotellei
Victor De Langhestraat
Lanteernhofstraat
Luchtvaartstraat
12
4
5
1
2
3
Arthur Matthyslaan
TE BOELAARPARK
Gitschotellei
Karel de Preterlei
Bikschotelaan
Berchemlei

N
W ← E
S
4,5 km

1 Arthur Matthyslaan 59
Hubert Semal
1966

2 Arthur Matthyslaan 61
Albert Poels
1940

3 Arthur Matthyslaan 63
Hubert Semal
1963

4 Smetsstraat 7
Lode Wouters
1961

5 Jozef Verbovenlei 121
Lode Wouters & Fons Mostien
1974

6 Muggenberglei 226
Walter Van den Broeck
1932

7 Ravelsbergstraat 12, 14, 46, 58

8 Van Notenstraat 7
Walter Van den Broeck
1932

9 Van Notenstraat 17
Nachman Kaplansky
1937

10 Wolfjagerslei 18
Eduard Van Steenbergen
1928

11 Cruyslei 1B
Albert Barentsen
1958

12 Luchtvaartstraat 28
Renaat Braem
1954

13 Boekenberglei 265
Eduard Van Steenbergen
1935

14 Eduard van Steenbergenlaan 27
Constant De Winter
1961

15 Eduard van Steenbergenlaan 42
Jan Jaak Jacobs
1958

16 Oudedonklaan
Eduard Van Steenbergen
1920s

17 Floralaan 7
Constant De Winter
1969

18 Menegemlei 23
Renaat Braem
1958

19 Boekenberglei 129
Roger Groothaert
1956

20 Boekenberglei 195
Hubert Semal
1970

21 Van Baurscheitlaan 16/18
Jules Eneman
1965

22 Van Baurscheitlaan 22
Paul Meekels
1965

23 Van Baurscheitlaan 24
unknown
1960s

24 Van Baurscheitlaan 60, 68
unknown
1960s

Deurne, a suburb with many faces, lies to the east of Antwerp's city centre. With dense working-class neighbourhoods and former castles that have been turned into public parks and tree-lined lanes with stately buildings, there's something here for everyone.

Deurne's population grew exponentially after both World Wars, which explains why there are so many modern buildings in such close proximity. The part we will be exploring on this tour borders on two lovely green spaces: Boekenbergpark (which has a swimming pond!) and Te Boelaerpark. This is a wonderful area to roam and several of the featured buildings are the homes of renowned architects – they were obviously on to something!

A little service announcement before we start: technically, the first three stops are in Borgerhout, but they are so worthwhile that we've decided to turn a blind eye.

Right near bus stop Borgerhout Te Boelaerlei on Arthur Matthyslaan you will find your very first stop: the home of Hubert Semal on no. 59 (**1**), with its delightfully colourful, 1960s façade. It is rather easy to miss because of the gorgeous conifer in the front yard, but it is definitely worth taking a closer look. Even more remarkable than the colours, perhaps, is the beautiful bas-relief, courtesy of the sculptor (and Semal's father-in-law) Albert Poels. Semal's father Paul was also an architect and a member of the first wave of modernism, during the interbellum. Many of the original interior details have been preserved, such as the built-in cabinets, spiral staircases, a fresco on the terrace wall, and a spectacular, decorative wall divider in the hallway. All this goes to show what a creative genius Semal was, and it's a shame that his work has stayed under the radar all this time.

1. Arthur Matthyslaan 59, Hubert Semal (1966)

Next on your route, and literally next door (**2**), is Poels's own home (his first, that is). Albert Poels was a man of many talents, it seems, because

Arthur Matthyslaan 59, Hubert Semal (1966)

he designed this house himself, in characteristic New Objectivity style. The contrast between the bricks and the tiles, and between the square and the circular shapes, is especially noteworthy and, thankfully, well-preserved.

Follow Arthur Matthyslaan to number 63 (**3**), which also belonged to the Poels family. The sculptor's second home and atelier was designed by Semal. Here again, it's worth noting how the two collaborated to create a stunning design with a striking, modern façade and a classic bas-relief on the second floor.

3. Arthur Matthyslaan 63, Hubert Semal (1963)

Walk along Arthur Matthyslaan, then take the next street on your right, Smetsstraat. It's easy to walk past this leafy alley, but it is all the more rewarding when you spot architect Lode Wouters's own house at number 7 (**4**). The building really stands out among the more run-of-the-mill houses that line the street. Although it has a rather conventional gabled roof, the rest of the façade is spectacularly progressive with its combination of brick and glass in a concrete structure, resulting in an abstract composition. But Wouters also designed most of the home's built-in furniture: the sideboard, bookshelves, tables, desks, cupboards and shelves, beds, and benches. The interior with its painted brick interior walls, plastered and painted ceilings, painted sliding doors, and glazed doors with wooden frames reflects the exterior brilliantly. Thankfully all this has been preserved and the house is now listed as a heritage building, meaning it cannot be altered.

4. Smetsstraat 7, Lode Wouters (1961)

Smetsstraat 7, Lode Wouters (1961)

Head back and take a right onto Jozef Verbovenlei, where you will run into another design by Wouters at no. 121 (**5**). Built almost 15 years after his own home in Smetsstraat, this is a more brutalist design, and you see that his style evolved over time.

Take the second street on your left, called Basseliersstraat. At the top of this street, turn right onto Muggenberglei. You'll soon spot number 226's spectacular façade (**6**). This house was designed by Walter Van den Broeck, a leading Antwerp architect during the 1930s, whose career (and life) was unfortunately cut short at age 40 due to illness. Van den Broeck also designed furniture, kitchens and interior decoration. He was the founder of *Bouwkunde* magazine (1924-25), in which he argued in favour of a socialist view of architecture and urban planning, relying on functionalism and standardisation to achieve comfortable, affordable housing. He never got to finish his own house (which, to be clear, isn't this one), but the furniture he designed for it has been preserved and is kept in storage by his daughter, who happens to live in Deurne. A signature element in his work are his window designs, of which you can see a nice example here. Fortunately, the wooden joinery has been preserved (or restored). Do check out the interaction between the door, the garage door, and the windows: so pleasing!

6. Muggenberglei 226, Walter Van den Broeck (1932)

Keep walking and turn right onto Ravelsbergstraat, which is like stepping back in time, as several of the interbellum façades on this street have been preserved. Numbers 12, 14, 46, and 58 (**7**) are particularly noteworthy.

Cross Jozef Verbovenlei to Van Notenstraat. Here, you can spot another Walter Van den Broeck gem at number 7 (**8**). Again, notice the windows, which are round rather than square in this instance.

Further along, at number 17 (**9**), you will come across a building by another leading architect of that era. Born in Poland and of Russian descent, Nachman Kaplansky moved to Antwerp from Tel Aviv in 1925, where he studied at the Royal Academy of Fine Arts. The client for whom he designed this house was a diamond dealer and clearly had a sizeable budget. Just look at that enormous bay window, which must have turned quite a few heads back in 1937. This project was just up Kaplansky's alley, as he loved to combine different materials such as exotic wood, lavish carpets, and decorative fabrics, to create colourful and unique universes. In that sense, he was very similar to Robert Mallet-Stevens, who designed Villa Cavrois in the north of France. Unfortunately, most of Kaplansky's interiors have either disappeared or have been renovated, including this one.

Take the next street on your right, Joos Robijnslei, and then turn left onto Wolfjagerslei.

This tour is starting to have all the makings of an all-star route of iconic Antwerp architects, and it kind of is. Eduard Van Steenbergen definitely ranks up there with the greatest and it's easy to spot the dwelling that he designed at number 18 (**10**). One of the defining features of Van Steenbergen's architecture was his use (and design) of stained-glass windows, as in this house.

10. Wolfjagerslei 18, Eduard Van Steenbergen (1928)

Keep walking and turn right onto Cruyslei. You'll find number 1B (**11**), the former home of Albert Barentsen which has since been turned into apartments, just before Te Boelaerpark. Barentsen and his architectural oeuvre are not very well-known. One thing we do know about him, however, is that he apprenticed with Kaplansky. It's a small world!

11. Cruyslei 1B, Albert Barentsen (1958)

Turn left onto Gitschotellei, then take the second street on your right, Luchtvaartstraat. At number 28, you will find a lesser-known Renaat Braem design (**12**).

Keep walking, then turn left onto Lanteernhofstraat. Before the merge with Jan Olieslagersstraat, turn right onto Boekenberglei, where you'll find another house by Eduard Van Steenbergen at number 265 (**13**). The difference with the house that you just walked past on Wolfjagerslei, could not be more striking, especially if you bear in mind that it was built just ten years later. Even today it still looks radically modern. The top floor was added in the 1960s by none other than Lode Wouters. In recent years, the house has undergone a welcome renovation, and the original design and colour of the façade have been restored. 13. Boekenberglei 265, Eduard Van Steenbergen (1935)

Turn back and walk up Boekenberglei towards Drakenhoflaan where you turn right, and then left onto Eduard Van Steenbergenlaan. This neighbourhood was built up after the Second World War and is like a time capsule of the Expo 58 era.

Boekenberglei 265, Eduard Van Steenbergen (1935)

The neatest and best-kept example can be found at number 27 (**14**) and is by Constant De Winter.

14. Eduard van Steenbergenlaan 27, Constant De Winter (1961)

No. 42 on the same street by Jan Jaak Jacobs (**15**) was built in 1958. Jacobs began his career in the 1930s and apprenticed with the iconic and acclaimed architect Léon Stynen, who introduced him to modernist architecture in all its facets.

15. Eduard van Steenbergenlaan 42, Jan Jaak Jacobs (1958)

Continue walking until Eduard Van Steenbergenlaan turns into Oudedonklaan (**16**). The uniformity of the houses on this street is apparent, which is the merit of Van Steenbergen. He was inspired by the British Arts & Crafts movement for his design for this neighbourhood, which spans many of the neighbouring streets. Much of Van Steenbergen's early output is in this style. Thanks to the amazing upkeep of these houses, it really feels as if you have stepped back in time.

Next, take the first street on your right, Floralaan. Number 7 (**17**), another design by Constant De Winter, has undergone some alterations (the most noticeable being the façade, originally made from fair-faced concrete which has since been painted white). Nonetheless, it is still a great example of late modernism, on the cusp of brutalism.

17. Floralaan 7, Constant De Winter (1969)

Turn back, walk in the direction of the park and take a right onto Unitaslaan, turning left at the end. Menegemlei 23 (**18**), the home that Renaat Braem designed for himself, is Deurne's best example of post-war modernism. From the street, the house appears rather unassuming, but just wait until you see the back, or even better, the interior. Braem made the decision to leave the house to the Flemish government after his death, to preserve it for the future. After an extensive restoration in the early 2000s, it became a museum, although it is still occupied. This may seem evident but to preserve literally everything – the architecture, the furniture, the decoration, ... – is actually quite remarkable and an exceptional tour de force. The interior includes seating by Arne Jacobsen and Osvaldo Borsani, tables designed by Braem and his wife, artist and graphic designer Elza Severin, and lighting by Angelo Ostuni, Hans-Agne Jakobsson, and Isamu Noguchi. Another striking element in the preserved interior is the couple's collection of traditional utensils and folk art in wood, glass, metal, and pottery, and a cornucopia of found objects, such as stones, fossils, and shells, which the couple collected during a lifetime of travelling the world. Braem's spirit is still very much present in the house, which he designed to feel at one with nature. The house was used for living and working, and Braem made optimal use of the green surroundings and the plot's orientation for these functions. This marriage between nature and architecture can be taken quite literally, as

Menegemlei 23, Renaat Braem (1958)

Menegemlei 23, Renaat Braem (1958)

the building originally also had a roof garden, which later had to be removed due to leaks.

18. Menegemlei 23, Renaat Braem (1958)

Take the second street on your left to walk back to Boekenberglei, where you can see another architect's home at no. 129. Roger Groothaert (**19**) was a strong believer in the integration of architecture and art, a vision he shared with Braem. Together they set up a working group on the subject, but it was disbanded soon after it was established. Groothaert still put his ideas into practice, though, designing buildings, as well as carpets, ceramics, furniture, posters, etc. 19. Boekenberglei 129, Roger Groothaert (1956)

Further down the street, at no. 195 (**20**), Hubert Semal makes a reappearance. We're in luck as this house was very recently restored, meaning the balcony railing was painted the original red again, among other things. 20. Boekenberglei 195, Hubert Semal (1970)

Walk back and turn right onto Flor Van Reethpad, to get to Van Baurscheitlaan. Go both left and right as there are so many wonderful 1960s dwellings that line what is perhaps the most beautiful street in this neighbourhood, particularly numbers 16/18 (**21**), 22 (**22**), 24 (**23**) and 60 and 68 (**24**).

24. Van Baurscheitlaan 60, unknown (1960s)

Turn around and walk back all the way to the end of Van Baurscheitlaan, then turn left on Gouverneur Holvoetlaan. Cross Boekenerglei to arrive at Cruyslei, where you'll find a tram stop.

Mechelen

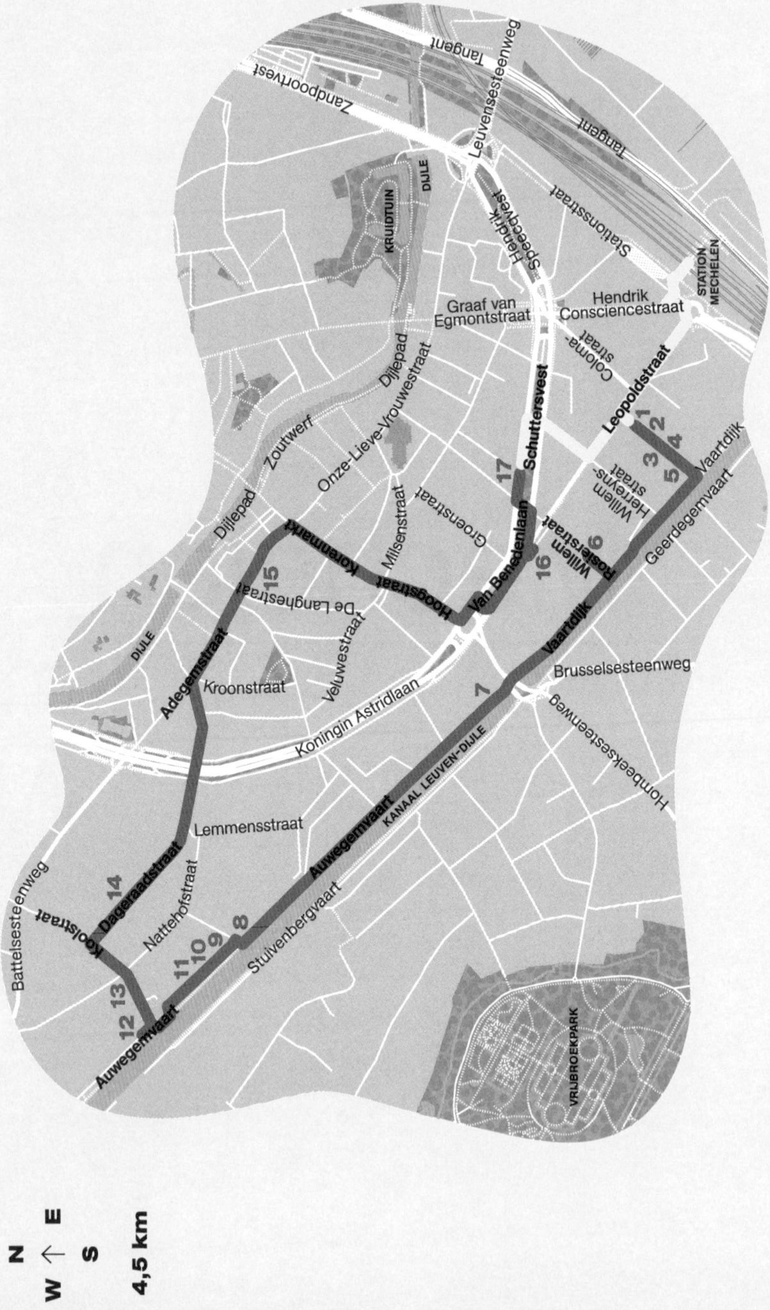
Tangent
Zandpoortvest
Leuvensesteenweg
Tangent
Stationsstraat
STATION MECHELEN
KRUIDTUIN
DIJLE
Hendrik Speecqvest
Graaf van Egmontstraat
Hendrik Consciencestraat
Coloma-straat
Leopoldstraat
Dijlepad
Onze-Lieve-Vrouwestraat
Zoutwerf
Schuttersvest
Willem Herreyns-straat
Vaartdijk
Dijlepad
Korenmarkt
Milsenstraat
Groenstraat
Van Benedenlaan
Willem Rosierstraat
Geerdegemvaart
Hoogstraat
De Langhestraat
DIJLE
Adegemstraat
Veluwestraat
Kroonstraat
Vaartdijk
Brusselsesteenweg
Koningin Astridlaan
Hombeeksesteenweg
KANAAL LEUVEN-DIJLE
Lemmensstraat
Auwegemvaart
Dageraadstraat
Battelsesteenweg
Nattehofstraat
Koolstraat
Stuivenbergvaart
Auwegemvaart
VRIJBROEKPARK
1
2
3
4
5
6
7
8
9
10
11
12
13
14
15
16
17
N
W E
S
4,5 km

1 Willem Geetsstraat 1
Jos Chabot
1938

2 Willem Geetsstraat 3
Jos Chabot
1938

3 Willem Geetsstraat 18
Cint Vermeulen
1930s

4 Willem Geetsstraat 26
unknown
1930s

5 Willem Geetsstraat 25
Jef Huygh
1925

6 Willem Rosierstraat 23
Alfons Roose
1930s

7 Auwegemvaart 7
R. Van Dijck
1935

8 Auwegemvaart 51
Roger De Winter
1950s-1960s

9 Auwegemvaart 56
Jos Chabot
1930

10 Auwegemvaart 58 & 59
J. Schaerlaken
1936

11 Auwegemvaart 70
Jos Chabot
1935

12 Auwegemvaart 83
Gaston Eysselinck
1934

13 Koolstraat 72
Jos Chabot
1934

14 Dageraadstraat 44
Jos Chabot
1934

15 Adegemstraat 31
Alfons Roose
1955

16 Van Benedenlaan 42
Jos Chabot
1939

17 Schuttersvest 7
Huib Hoste
1935

Once upon a time, Mechelen was a prosperous city and an economic powerhouse. In the 16th century, under Margaret of Austria, it briefly was the capital of the Low Countries (the present-day Netherlands, Belgium, and Luxembourg). In the 19th century, Mechelen and Brussels were the first cities on the continent to be connected by a railway, making Mechelen a hub in the European railway network and allowing for all kinds of industrial activity.

By the start of the "Modern Movement", Mechelen had become a languishing (in economic terms) provincial town – not the best breeding ground for the radical new architecture that was sprouting up elsewhere. However, the interbellum period produced some interesting architects who worked in a regional style, and this route focusses on their output, taking you on a trip through the 1930s for the most part.

Exit Mechelen's train station through the main entrance, walk left towards the roundabout, and down the wide street that leads into the city centre, Leopoldstraat. Next, take the second street on your left, Willem Geetsstraat. After the First World War, the city built several new neighbourhoods, and this street is part of one of them. What makes Willem Geetsstraat remarkable is that most of its interbellum buildings have been preserved (despite not being listed). But what's even more remarkable: at number 1 (**1**) you find the former home and office of Jos Chabot, who just happens to be the most important figure in interbellum modernism in Mechelen. A job for one wealthy local led to many others for the regional bourgeoisie.

1. Willem Geetsstraat 1, Jos Chabot (1938)

After graduating in 1923, Chabot went to work for Edward Van Not, who designed most of the buildings on Cogels-Osylei in Antwerp, a street that is famed for its majestic art nouveau architecture. He later met younger modern architects such as Léon Stynen, for whom he designed the bedroom of the decorative arts pavilion for the 1930 world fair in Antwerp. Chabot would also co-design the Gevaert pavilion for that same world fair. From 1932 onwards, as a result of a partnership with the Jacobs brewery, Chabot's designs popped all over Mechelen. A household name in Mechelen, the brewery owned several cafes, for which they asked Chabot to design the exteriors. You'll walk past one of them later on this route, but sadly most of these pubs have either disappeared or have been completely butchered.

Back to the here and now and Willem Geetsstraat 1. Chabot designed this block of flats in 1934. His home and office were located on the ground floor. Although the joinery has been renewed, the façade's original look, with its curved edges and ditto windows, has been preserved. Look closely, however, and you can spot a stained-glass window by Chabot above the entrance, a trademark element in most of the houses that he designed. A visionary and a perfectionist, the more Chabot was allowed to design, the better. Gardens, furniture, textiles, … Chabot was happy to work on them all. He once even designed a bathing suit for his daughter.

Just next door, at number 3 (**2**), you'll find a more toned-down example of his work, leaning towards the functionalism of the New Objectivity style.

2. Willem Geetsstraat 3, Jos Chabot (1938)

Number 18 (**3**) was designed in a similar vein and was recently renovated. The façade was cleaned and the joinery renewed and painted black instead of white, to underscore its New Objectivity design.

3. Willem Geetsstraat 18, Cint Vermeulen (1930s)

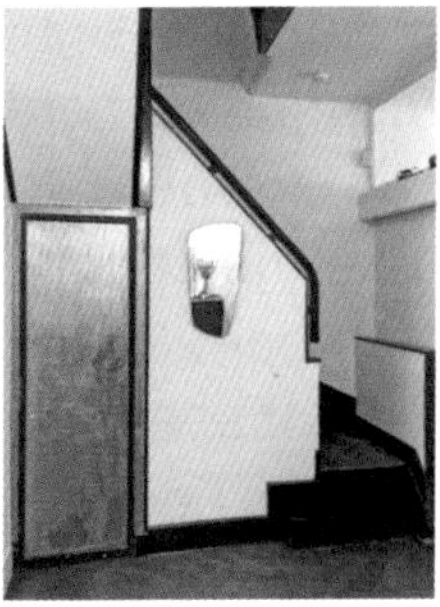

A last gem that you can't afford to miss on this street is the one at number 26 (**4**). Check out the beautiful stained-glass above, and the graphic grille on the door. Unfortunately, the renewed joinery detracts from the simple art deco style that characterises this block of flats.

4. Willem Geetsstraat 26, unknown (1930s)

Across the street at number 25 (**5**) you'll find number 26's less unassuming relative: a house in the sort of ornamental art deco style that you rarely see in Belgium but which would fit in seamlessly in Austria, as it is reminiscent of the Vienna Secession style that originated there.

Although there are several other noteworthy examples of modernism on this street, most have undergone significant alterations so are not worth mentioning here. Continue walking to the end of the street, where you turn right onto Vaartdijk, and then take the second on your right, Willem Rosierstraat. Number 23 (**6**) should immediately stand out, as it's not every day that you come across a pink tiled façade. Featuring a semi-circular glass bay window, a built-in terrace, and the typical solarium with a pergola on the top floor, this house is all about the quality of living. All this will hopefully help you overlook the unseemly new, thick PVC window frames.

6. Willem Rosierstraat 23, Alfons Roose (1930s)

Walk back to Vaartdijk and turn right, with the water to your left. Head to Auwegemvaart and stop at number 7 (**7**). By combining different materials and shapes (check out the gorgeous curved fencing that frames the steps to the entrance), architect Van Dijck (the initial R is all that's known of his first name) managed to add several interesting details to an otherwise minimalist façade.

7. Auwegemvaart 7, R. Van Dijck (1935)

Now it's time for a bit of a walk until you reach number 51 (**8**), an interesting post-war building by Roger De Winter. Although De Winter made quite a name for himself after the Second World War, little is known about this dwelling, other than that the façade's colour scheme has been altered. Despite this, it's still gorgeous! 8. Auwegemvaart 51, Roger De Winter (1950s-1960s)

Just five doors down at number 56, you will find a welcome change from the single-family dwellings that you've come across so far: a canoe club from 1930 by Jos Chabot (**9**). The original, red four-panel door with its porthole windows refers to the ocean liners of that era: luxurious ships with curved shapes, horizontal lines and nautical elements. This style is called Streamline Moderne (or Paquebot in French), and given the fact that Chabot designed this building for a canoe club, it's perfectly fitting. 9. Auwegemvaart 56, Jos Chabot (1930)

At numbers 58 and 59, you'll find a pretty double dwelling (**10**). Apart from the renewed joinery, most of its characteristic details have been preserved, including the cimorné wall cladding, the columns, and the beautiful doors.

10. Auwegemvaart 58 & 59, J. Schaerlaken (1936)

Continue your walk and stop at number 70 (**11**), where yet another Chabot awaits. Like his canoe club, this house is another great example of the Streamline Moderne style. Check out the porthole windows, the curved railings, the horizontal lines, and the monumental windows. Even though it's partly obscured by greenery, you can't miss the striking stained glass near the entrance, depicting an ocean view, behind which the stairwell is located. The interior has also been beautifully preserved. The house has been listed as heritage, meaning it cannot be altered, both on the in- and outside.

11. Auwegemvaart 70, Jos Chabot (1935)

From one great house to the next: walk to the top of Auwegemvaart, then up the little dirt road to get back to the embankment and check out number 83 (**12**): a home designed in 1934 by none other than Gaston Eysselinck, one of the pioneers of Belgian modernism. On the right-hand side of number 83, on the corner (Koolstraat 102), you'll find another building by Eysselinck. Initially, these two houses were conceived as one building, for the writer and progressive socialist Albert van Hoogenbemt, but the plot was later divided into two. The plans also included a structure on pilotis (freestanding columns), but this was never built. These elements, and the use of reinforced concrete, are clearly inspired by Le Corbusier's Weissenhof Estate in Stuttgart. At the time, reinforced concrete was so innovative that builders didn't quite know how to use it yet. This soon resulted in visible wear and tear. The whole debacle led to heated discussions between van Hoogenbemt (who lived at 102) and Eysselinck. The situation was finally settled with some help from the architect Huib Hoste, who wanted to prevent this minor setback from casting a shadow on modern architecture. Ultimately, both owners altered their façades. While 102 was clad in white plaster, 83 got a decorative, brick façade. In time, the interiors were extensively renovated, causing them to stray from Eysselinck's initial vision.

12. Auwegemvaart 83, Gaston Eysselinck (1934)

Walk down Koolstraat, where numbers 100 to 72 are all by Chabot. Number 72 (**13**) has been partly renovated, but the stained-glass window which references the Jacobs brewery is still in place.

13. Koolstraat 72, Jos Chabot (1934)

For more designs by Chabot, continue walking down Koolstraat and turn right onto Dageraadstraat, to number 44 (**14**). By now, you've seen a nice selection of his work and yet, he still has a trick or two up his sleeve. The yellow brickwork with shadow joints (also named Dudok joints, after the Dutch architect Willem Dudok who made extensive use of them), the simple yet graphic stained-glass, the porthole windows, and of course the curved forms, are simply stunning.

14. Dageraadstraat 44, Jos Chabot (1934)

Dageraadstraat 44, Jos Chabot (1934)

Follow Dageraadstraat until it turns into Monseigneur Van Nuffelstraat, cross the ring road (Koningin Astridlaan) and head to Korte Heistraat, where you take the second street on your right, Adegemstraat. At number 31 (**15**) you can find the second and last post-war building on this tour. Alfons Roose was part of both the first (interbellum) and second (post-war) wave of modernism, and he excelled during both. This was his own home and as you can see, Roose had an eye for detail. From the sculpture of an architect next to the door, over the striped canopy, to the little sculptures on top – there's so much to discover here. As you might have guessed, Roose's imagination did not stop at the exterior; he also designed the interior and the furniture. Today you can still see some of the original furniture at Museum Hof Van Busleyden.

15. Adegemstraat 31, Alfons Roose (1955)

Take the next street on your right, Korenmarkt, which turns into Hoogstraat, and walk to the end. Cross the ring road (Van Benedenlaan) and walk left until you get to number 42 (**16**), another house by Jos Chabot. The façade is almost as classical as it is modern. This can be explained by the origins of this house: the original clients were manufacturers of Flemish neo-renaissance furniture – not exactly something you would associate with modernism. Inside there are state-of-the-art hidden ceiling lights, combined with a heavy wooden staircase and stained-glass windows that depict classical Flemish artworks.

16. Van Benedenlaan 42, Jos Chabot (1939)

Your tour ends with what's probably the highlight of this entire walk: House Lens (named after its owner, the lawyer Joris Lens) by Huib Hoste, one of the greats of the modernist movement in Belgium. With your back to Van Benedenlaan 42, turn right and walk to the zebra crossing and cross the ring road (now Schuttersvest) again and walk right. You can find House Lens at number 7 (**17**). Have a good look at the façade and try to notice anything that looks out of the ordinary. Perhaps you may have noticed, or perhaps you didn't, but the first and second floors are not aligned with the street. Instead, they are set at an angle, facing south. A typical feature of modernism consists of concealing the building materials used, which is why, in Corbusian fashion, this façade was covered with granito and then painted white. Given the relative minimalism of the exterior you may be surprised to know that Hoste also had an eye for playful aesthetics. This is apparent from the entrance, for example, which features terra cotta tiles and beautiful woodwork and ironwork on the doors. Once inside, it feels as if you've travelled back in time, as literally everything has been restored to meticulous detail. Thank God for passionate owners like these, who protect and preserve the spirit of modernism, even if this means having to compromise on modern comforts.

17. Schuttersvest 7, Huib Hoste (1935)

To walk back to the train station, take the next street on your right, Albert Geudensstraat, then turn left onto Leopoldstraat, and the station will loom up in front of you.

Heysel (Brussels)

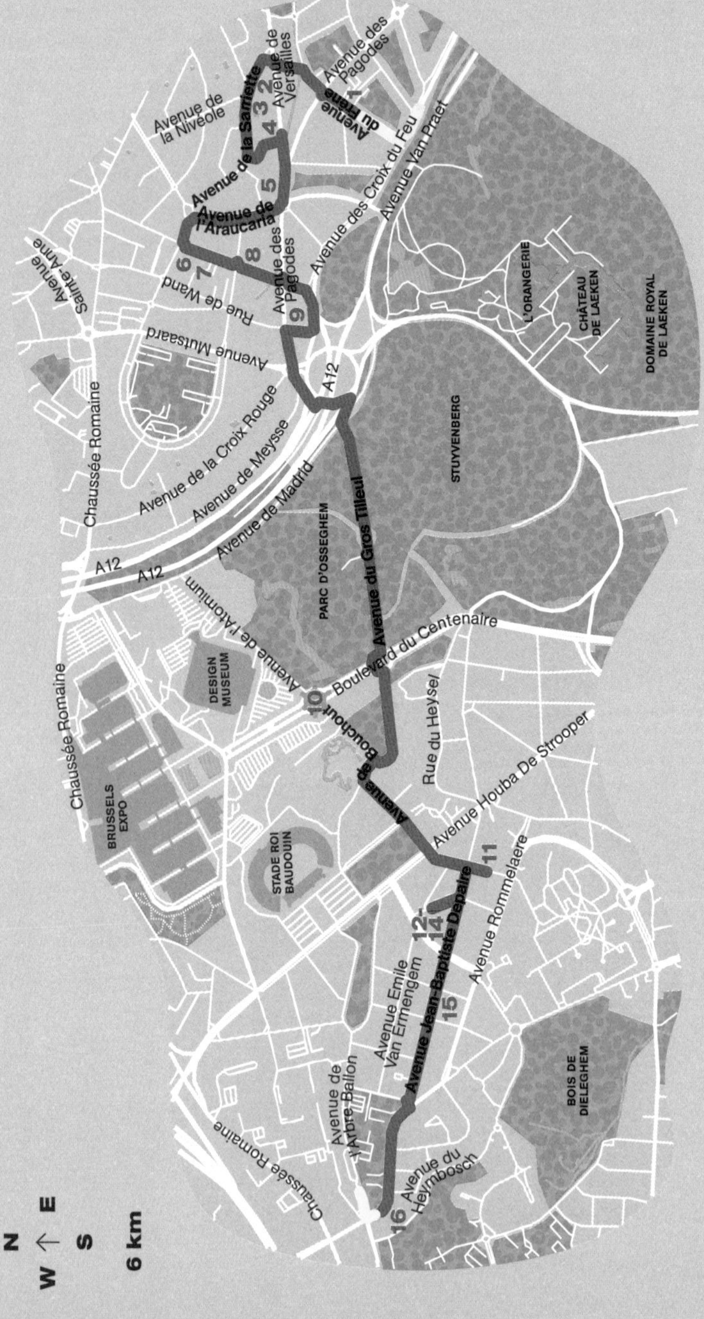
Avenue des Pagodes
Avenue de Versailles
Avenue du Frêne
Avenue de la Sarriette
Avenue de la Nivéole
Avenue de l'Araucaria
Avenue des Croix du Feu
Avenue Van Praet
Avenue Sainte-Anne
Rue de Wand
Avenue des Pagodes
Avenue Mutsaard
L'ORANGERIE
CHÂTEAU DE LAEKEN
DOMAINE ROYAL DE LAEKEN
A12
Chaussée Romaine
Avenue de la Croix Rouge
Avenue de Meysse
Avenue de Madrid
STUYVENBERG
PARC D'OSSEGHEM
Avenue du Gros Tilleul
A12
A12
Avenue de l'Atomium
Boulevard du Centenaire
DESIGN MUSEUM
Chaussée Romaine
Avenue de Bouchout
Rue du Heysel
Avenue Houba De Strooper
BRUSSELS EXPO
STADE ROI BAUDOUIN
Avenue Rommelaere
Avenue Jean-Baptiste Depaire
Avenue Emile Van Ermengem
Avenue de l'Arbre Ballon
BOIS DE DIELEGHEM
Chaussée Romaine
Avenue du Heymbosch
1
2
3
4
5
6
7
8
9
10
11
12-14
15
16
N
W
E
S
6 km

1 Avenue du Frêne 55
Marcel Winckel
1955

2 Avenue de la Sarriette 91
Joseph Massin
1960

3 Avenue de la Sarriette 83
C. Belen
1961

4 Avenue de Versailles 48
Roger De Winter
1962

5 Avenue de Versailles 14
Georges Pepermans
1959

6 Avenue Jean de Bologne 66
Marcel Winckel
1960

7 Avenue Jean de Bologne 62
Willy Van Der Meeren
1962

8 Avenue de Busleyden 37
J. Degand en H. Guchez
1958

9 Avenue des Croix du Feu 301, 303
Louis Tenaerts
1937

10 Atomium, Place de l'Atomium
Jean & André Polak
1958

11 Avenue Edouard Kufferath 42
Liévin Van Labeke
1949

12 Avenue Adrien Bayet 11
Willy Van Der Meeren
1952

13 Avenue Jean-Baptiste Depaire 81
Janssen
1936

14 Avenue Jean-Baptiste Depaire 83
unknown
1930s

15 Avenue Jean-Baptiste Depaire 160
Jean-François Van Immelen, H. Leyers
1958

16 Avenue Joseph De Heyn 120-136
1950s-1960s

The area in Laeken (part of Brussels) that is known as "Heysel" at one time was the centre of Expo 58. This first world fair in Belgium after the Second World War had an optimistic theme, namely "A World for a Better Life for Mankind", referring to the confidence and faith in progress thanks to engineering and science. As a result, the fair featured several very original pavilions, where the latest developments in construction techniques (the Atomium, anyone?) were applied. Although many of the pavilions have since disappeared, they had a lasting influence on the architecture of that era. So get ready for a wild ride past some of the best of this architecture, with a couple of 1930s interbellum dwellings thrown in for good measure.

Good to know: this is a long tour that can easily be split into two trips, with the first ending at number 9 and the second starting at number 10, the Atomium.

Get off the tram at Buissonnets, walk up Avenue des Croix du Feu, with the park on your left. Take the second street on your right, Avenue du Frêne, and walk to number 55 (**1**). This house with its wooden panelling and a playful terrace on the second floor is your first taste of the 1950s aesthetic.

Follow the street to the roundabout and continue walking straight on, by taking the second exit onto Rue de Beyseghem, after which you turn left onto Avenue de la Sarriette. This narrow street temporarily becomes a footpath. Cross Avenue de Versailles and stay on Avenue de la Sarriette. Stop at number 91 (**2**). How can you not smile when you see this house? Feast your eyes on the asymmetrical shape, the interaction between different materials, and the colourful doors. The interior, with its blue mosaic floors and graphic spiral staircase, is just as cheerful.

2. Avenue de la Sarriette 91, Joseph Massin (1960)

The house down the road, at number 83 (**3**), has a more radical design, but ultimately it was built in the same spirit. Butterfly roofs are a recurring motif in mid-century modernism, of which you can see an example here. In addition to looking neat, these roofs are also functional: the inversion of the typical gable roof shape allows for higher exterior walls, which – when combined with windows – let in more light. The wide overhangs also act as canopies: in summer, when the sun is high in the sky, they provide shade for the building (in winter, meanwhile, the low-hanging winter sun can just filter in). So smart! This house's roof isn't the only eye-catcher, however: check out the stairs that lead to the entrance, and the graphic chimney.

3. Avenue de la Sarriette 83, C. Belen (1961)

Continue walking down Avenue de la Sarriette, then turn left onto Drève du Long Bonnier and walk to the corner with Avenue de Versailles, where you can find your next stop on your left: Villa Zonnewende (**4**) by Roger De Winter. Check out the beautiful original typography of the house's name, which is Dutch for "solstice". The name is hardly surprising as the house is drenched in light. As you may have noticed, it is situated on a slope, causing the bedrooms at the rear to be aligned with the garden level. As was De Winter's custom, he also designed much of the interior, which has been preserved.

With your back to the villa and Drève du Long Bonnier, turn right onto Avenue de Versailles until you reach number 14 (**5**). Talk about sunlight streaming in! Glass was a common denominator in most post-war modernist architecture. As a material, glass by then was much more diverse and stronger, becoming a building material in its own right. While the trend of letting in light wasn't new in modernism, architects definitely took it to a whole new level after the Second World War. In their quest for maximum light, architects moved the load-bearing walls to the interior, and used monumental panes of glass for the exterior walls. This definitely increased the energy consumption of these houses, but since heating costs were at an all-time low and climate change was not a hot topic in those days, it really wasn't considered an issue at the time. These days, however, poor insulation and energy efficiency pose a major threat to modernist heritage. They are a driving factor behind many renovations of modernist houses, often driving a stake through their lovely appearance (think thick PVC window profiles instead of thin steel ones).

5. Avenue de Versailles 14, Georges Pepermans (1959)

Walk to the roundabout, where you turn right onto Avenue de l'Araucaria, then left onto Avenue Wannecouter, which leads to another roundabout. Here, turn left onto Avenue Jean de Bologne. Your next stop is very near, at number 66 on your right (**6**). This house was designed by Marcel Winckel, who built several similar dwellings in this area, including his own home. Although the design isn't too radical, it's still a nice example of the post-war style, incorporating many of its typical elements: playful railing on the stairs, the use of concrete and natural stone, and Glasal panels.

Just two doors down at number 62 (**7**) lies an absolutely remarkable house by Willy Van Der Meeren. Here too, you can spot several elements that are typical of post-war modernism. Originally the house was built for a photographer, who had his studio in the cellar and his showroom on the ground floor. This explains the large shop window in the front: in those days, nobody "lived" here. When the current owners bought the house, Van Der Meeren's design had already been altered. Fortunately, they took it upon themselves to restore it to its original condition. The front show-room – which has now been converted into living space – is separated from the (other) living spaces by a door, behind which a small set of stairs takes you to a mezzanine that overlooks the garden. Another set of stairs takes you to the living room floor (with a nice fireplace) and the kitchen, which also overlooks the garden. The bedrooms and the bathroom are on the floor above. The rear façade mirrors the front façade, with windows set in a concrete structure. 7. Avenue Jean de Bologne 62, Willy Van Der Meeren (1962)

Avenue Jean de Bologne 62, Willy Van Der Meeren (1962)

Take a left onto Avenue de Busleyden, and walk to number 37 (**8**). By now, you must recognise that optimistic post-war style a mile away. Here you will see “more of the same”, but nobody ever turned down the opportunity to admire some joy, surely?

Good news for those who believe that variation is the spice of life: the next stop will take you back in time, to the interbellum! Walk back to the round-about, but this time turn left onto Avenue Jean de Bologne and walk all the way down to Avenue des Croix du Feu, where you turn right, and walk to numbers 301 and 303 (**9**). Though both these dwellings are by Louis Tenaerts and they were built in the same year, they couldn’t be further apart. Number 301, with its subtle Streamline Moderne elements (in moderation), is a true modernist design, while number 303 goes all-out art deco with its lavish ornamentation. It’s fun to note that Tenaerts couldn’t resist adding just one tiny decorative element to the façade of 301: a sculpture of two birds. See if you can spot it!

9. Avenue des Croix du Feu 303, 301, Louis Tenaerts (1937)

Walk down Avenue des Croix du Feu, which bends to the right and becomes Rue de Wand. Right before the intersection with Avenue des Pagodes, you should see a public toilet on your left, with a path right next to it. Walk down the path. Pass underneath the bridge. At the end, you should be able to turn left and walk underneath another bridge. Enter the pedestrian tunnel behind it. Once out of the tunnel, walk under two more bridges and after the second one, walk into the pedestrian tunnel on your right. At the other end of the tunnel, you should see the former American pavilion for Expo 58, which was designed by the American (duh!) architect Edward Durell Stone, loom up ahead. The building originally consisted of three interconnected cylinders, but was later heavily altered. Very little remains of the original design. Walk into the park along Avenue du Gros Tilleul where the most iconic remnant of Expo 58 will come into view: the jaw-dropping Atomium (**10**)! Belgians often fail to appreciate this absolutely smashing structure, that seems to defy the rules of design and construction. What is perhaps even more remarkable is that it still stands here today, in all its glory. And it has withstood the test of time in superb fashion (and with some renovation). Go straight at the roundabout and continue down Avenue du Gros Tilleul. At the next roundabout, to your right, you should have a clear view of the nine balls of shiny steel that form the Atomium. Take some time to take a closer look at it and then go straight at the roundabout and follow Avenue du Gros Tilleul. After the bend to the right, take a left at the intersection onto Avenue de Bouchout, and then immediately turn left again to stay on the same street.

Cross Avenue Houba De Strooper and walk up Avenue Edouard Kufferath, where you stop at number 42 (**11**). In terms of style, this house by Liévin Van Labeke which he designed for himself in 1949, straddles the interbellum and post-war modernism. The protruding, round bay window and the terrace with its ornamental railing are especially noteworthy.

Walk back, then turn left onto Avenue Jean-Baptiste Depaire, and then right onto Avenue Adrien Bayet. Walk to number 11 (**12**). More Willy Van Der Meeren! This house, which was built ten years before the one in Avenue Jean de Bologne and six years before Expo 58, is remarkably radical. Fortunately, the façade was recently restored. When the current owners bought it, the house looked rather rundown. Thanks to their meticulous restoration, it's as good as new again. In typical Van Der Meeren fashion, the interior features built-in furniture, of which the partitioning wall/cabinet is the absolute highlight. Van Der Meeren used colour throughout the house, but it really comes into its own in the kitchen, with a combination of blue, yellow, white, grey and black.

12. Avenue Adrien Bayet 11, Willy Van Der Meeren (1952)

Avenue Adrien Bayet 11, Willy Van Der Meeren (1952)

Avenue Adrien Bayet 11, Willy Van Der Meeren (1952)

Avenue Adrien Bayet 11, Willy Van Der Meeren (1952)

Walk back, then turn right onto Avenue Jean-Baptiste Depaire again, stopping at numbers 81 (**13**) and 83 (**14**) for the route's final examples of interbellum architecture. While they are side by side, they represent a completely different aspect of modernist architecture. Number 83 is a big, fat wedding of art deco and the Amsterdam School, featuring alternate brickwork and colourful iron-work. Number 81, on the other hand, is a bit showy but in a very subtle way. But the devil is in the detail: the recessed door, the minimalist ironwork on the door and garage, the cimorné that adorns the ground-floor façade, the mosaics on the columns around the windows, the elegant house number, and the tiny stained-glass window to the left of the front door.

13. Avenue Jean-Baptiste Depaire 81, Janssen (1936)

14. Avenue Jean-Baptiste Depaire 83, unknown (1930s)

On to number 160 (**15**), up the street. Alas, the joinery has been replaced but thankfully the rest has remained as it was. The abstract enamel artwork to the left of the front door is unique. It was created (and signed) by Walter De Buck, a sculptor from Ghent who often worked with mid-century architects. The combination of art and architecture as such wasn't that groundbreaking in the 1950s, but as a style in and of itself, it gained momentum during the post-war period. It manifested itself in many ways, such as ceramic or mosaic artworks, metal reliefs, stained-glass windows, sculptures, etc. Though the names of many of these artists were lost over time, the more notable architects easily found their way to equally famous artists. These artworks were always an integral part of the architectural designs.

15. Avenue Jean-Baptiste Depaire 160, Jean-François Van Immelen, H. Leyers (1958)

Walk to the end of Avenue Jean-Baptiste Depaire. At the intersection, turn right onto Avenue Joseph De Heyn. Here, you should take a closer look at numbers 120 through 136 (**16**), a fine ensemble of houses in a similar style. They're "more of the same", but not really – because there is a certain tension between conformity and novelty. This particular and innovative style developed into a trend in its own right over time. 16. Avenue Joseph De Heyn 120-136 (1950s-1960s)

The houses you've seen today indicate that the Expo 58 period was an era of fun and cheerful designs, which reflected the optimistic view of the future that people still had back then. It's both sad and interesting that it's precisely these qualities that caused people to not take this style very seriously, and even deride it. It probably doesn't help that many of the used materials and techniques haven't aged well and that rising energy costs are pushing the owners of these houses to renovate them. In recent years, though, the aesthetic has seen a bit of a revival. Hopefully this will lead to a reassessment – along with this walking guide, of course!

To get to tram stop De Heyn, walk down Avenue Joseph De Heyn and turn right onto Avenue de l'Arbre Ballon.

When I started this adventure in 2021, I had no idea where this book would lead me, or who I'd meet along the way. Two years later, all I can do is express my eternal gratitude.

Thank you to Niels, my partner in (and out of) crime, for all things text and for your never-wavering support. Thank you also to Chloé, the best friend anyone could ask for, and also the best graphic designer, for this beautiful book. Thank you to Marc and everyone at Luster for your trust, your boundless enthusiasm and that final push – I don't think I would've even considered writing a book were it not for your request. Thank you to everyone who opened their homes to me, and for all the warmth that I encountered during my visits.

Thank you to my parents, for being my biggest fans from the outset. Thank you to Helena for telling me to take Toerist Modernist seriously and for helping me to turn it into a "job". Thanks also to Laura aka Keppe for sharing all that information and enthusiasm about your grandfather, Louis Geirnaert. Thank you to the other members of the best non-profit organisation in town:

Maarten, Nel, and Femke. Thank you to Stefi of Modernist Estates, with whom I collaborated on my very first walking guide of Uccle, for trusting me. Thank you to Sofie for showing me around Brussels and planting the seed for what would one day become Toerist Modernist all those years ago. Thank you to the people of Erfgoed Vlaanderen: Julie, Jef, Sarah, and Caroline. Thank you to Rik for letting me stay in your home, the magical Schellekens house. Thank you to Xavier for showing me around Kortrijk. Thank you to all the volunteers who took this book for a test run: Bart and Jolien, Sara and Laura, Géraldine, Tine and Marc, Eva, Wout, Nicolas, Karlien and Magalie.

And of course, thank you, dear reader, for taking an interest in what I do!

Toerist Modernist
Walking along modernist architecture in Belgium

Concept and composing
Gerlin Heestermans
Final editing
Sandy Logan and Louise Vanderputte

Graphic Design
Chloé D'hauwe
Images
Gerlin Heestermans

D/2023/12.005/7
ISBN 9789460583438

lusterpublishing.com
info@lusterpublishing.com